P1

Love at t

M000085202

"*Love at the Speed of Email* is part grand romance, part travel memoir and part essay on life's most precious gifts. Lisa McKay is a phenomenal writer; clever and comedic, poignant and pitch-perfect. You will love this love story."

- Susan Meissner, award-winning author of *The Shape of Mercy* and *A Sound Among the Trees*

"*Love at the Speed of Email*, Lisa McKay's engrossing memoir about life and love and home, is a wild ride that spans the globe. At turns funny, contemplative, and romantic, Lisa's story resonated on many different levels and kept me eagerly turning pages, hoping for a happily-ever-after ending to this modern day fairy tale. I can't recommend this extraordinary book highly enough!"

- Nicole Baart, bestselling author of *Far From Here* and *After the Leaves Fall*

"A travel memoir with a deep soul, *Love at the Speed of Email* takes us around the world but always brings us back to the heart of the matter: humanity's longing for place, purpose, faith. Lisa McKay's seamless storytelling helps us find ourselves in every corner of her globetrotting and even learn a little about love along the way. A true pleasure for the journeyer in all of us!"

- Leeana Tankersley, author of *Found Art: Discovering Beauty in Foreign Places*

"*Love at the Speed of Email* is a riveting memoir by a talented author and globe-trotter. I loved journeying with Lisa McKay as she sought the love of her life and a place to call home. I can't recommend this beautiful and triumphant story enough!"

- Gina Holmes, award-winning author of *Crossing Oceans* and *Dry as Rain*

LOVE
at the SPEED
of EMAIL

Lisa McKay

Karinya Publishing
ISBN-13: 978-0-9854809-0-5

Cover design: Kimberly Glyder
Layout design: Ross Burck
Author photograph: Kevin McIntyre
Photograph of Michael Wolfe and Lisa McKay: Tristan Clements

For Mike, who wrote a letter and changed my life

CONTENTS

Los Angeles – Accra – Washington, D.C. – Sydney – Zagreb – South Bend – Nairobi – San Diego – Atlanta – Madang – Kona – Canberra – London – Baltimore – Itonga – Vancouver – Harare – Dushanbe – Lira – Petats – Port Moresby – Brisbane – Ballina - Malibu

SPINSTERS ABROAD

Los Angeles, USA

ALMOST TWO WEEKS AFTER my thirty-first birthday, the alarm on my mobile phone went off several hours earlier than normal. It was still dark when I opened my eyes, and as I groped for the phone I was seized by the sudden and horrible conviction that I had entirely forgotten I was supposed to be getting up and going to the airport.

This, I realized, could be worse than the time I booked my ticket to New York for the week *before* I needed to leave. It could be worse than the time I traveled to Colorado before discovering that I'd left my wallet in my gym bag at home. Surely, though, it couldn't be worse than the time I was stranded in Germany for a week because I'd neglected to get a visa for the Czech Republic. Could it?

When I finally managed to illuminate the screen on my phone, a *Task* list was displayed. There was only one item on it.

That item was *Lisa's wedding (Australia)*.

This did not immediately clarify things for me.

If the phone alarm was going off that early, I reasoned, still sleep-fuzzed, I was supposed to be going somewhere. According to my *To Do* list, however, that somewhere was Australia. For my own wedding.

Except ... I was having a hard time recollecting ever planning a wedding in Australia.

Or remembering who I might conceivably be marrying.

Then, slowly, it came back to me.

Two years earlier, I had been sitting in a California theater waiting for the movie to start. One of my good friends, Robin, had just gotten engaged. She was talking weddings and bemoaning the twin hassles of setting a date and finding a venue. I had constructively suggested that a lot of time and angst could perhaps be saved if you settled those details before you were even in a relationship. In response to her answering challenge to do just that for myself I had named a place (Australia, the closest thing to a home country I have) and a safely distant date.

Laughing like a loon, Robin had commandeered my phone and programmed in my wedding date for me, complete with an alarm reminder to get engaged three months before the actual day.

"No worries," I had said loftily when she explained what she was doing. "Three months will be plenty of time to plan a wedding."

Now, three months before that safely distant date, I groaned and silenced that alarm. Whatever had possessed her to think I'd want to start planning said wedding at 5 a.m. on a Friday, I wasn't sure.

ONE OF JANE AUSTEN'S most famous novels opens with this sentence: "It is a truth universally acknowledged, that a single man in possession of a good fortune, must be in want of a wife." Now two weeks past the landmark of thirty-one I was starting to wonder whether it was also a truth even more universally acknowledged that a single woman of a certain age and in possession of no fortune of which to speak must be in want of a husband.

Many of my friends and family certainly seemed to think so – this was not the first time in recent history that I had been ambushed at an early hour regarding the pressing matter of my nuptials. Even total strangers in African airports were in agreement on this point.

Accra, Ghana

THE INTERLUDE WITH THE stranger in Ghana came first.

I was sitting alone at dawn on a cold metal bench in Accra airport, reading, when he sat down beside me.

He was tall – that was the first thing I noticed. Easily six-eight, he towered over everyone else in a room that was already full of tall men. His skin was so shiny black, like oiled coal, that the fluorescent light glanced off him at odd angles. His hair was sectioned and bound into a dozen spiky knobs. He wore spotless red and white Nike exercise gear and sported an enormous square diamond in his left ear. He pulled out a portable DVD player and slid in a disc.

He waited longer than most, four minutes, before striking up a conversation.

"I am Gabriel," he said. "What is your name?"

I looked up from my book and sighed mentally.

"Lisa."

"Where are you going?"

"Nairobi."

"Why?"

"Work."

"What work?"

"I run workshops on stress, trauma, and resilience for humanitarian relief and development workers."

I could see that this last sentence didn't register, and I wasn't surprised. It usually took some time for native English speakers to fit those pieces together, and Gabriel spoke English with a thick West African-French accent.

"What do *you* do?" I said, wondering, as always, what was compelling me to ask this.

It's not that I wasn't interested in what he did – I was especially curious as to where the diamond came from. It was just that I didn't particularly want to end up chatting at length to yet another strange man in an airport in Africa. But no matter how many times I tell myself that I'm not responsible for reciprocating interest in situations like these, it breaks all the normal rules of polite behavior to give a one-word answer to a question and return my eyes to my book. Five questions is about my limit. After that I usually buckle and return one.

I learned that Gabriel was a seaman, working cargo ships out of Djibouti. His family was from Cote D'Ivoire but now lived in Ghana. English was his fourth language, and his worst.

"Are you married?" Gabriel asked me. "Do you have a boyfriend?"

This is why I don't enjoy chatting with men in airports in Africa.

"I have a boyfriend," I lied shamelessly.

Gabriel did not even pause. This was something I'd noticed with other men, too. Apparently, if my boyfriend was allowing me to wander around Africa unsupervised, I was fair game.

"Do you like to make friends with the black man?" he asked. "I know some white woman; they do not like to make friends with the black man."

Flummoxed, I tried to think. Answering no was out of the question. Answering yes was tantamount to an open invitation to continue this line of questioning.

I recalled the face of an ex-boyfriend and mentally grafted it onto my hypothetical current boyfriend.

"My boyfriend is black," I said.

Gabriel smiled. "I like to make friends with the white woman."

I looked down at my book and turned the page.

I have received more attention from men in Africa than anywhere else in the world. Most of the time, however, I don't think it's because of my sparkling personality. How sparkling can you be when you're travel-weary in an airport, especially when you're engrossed in a book? But I'm also not deluded enough to think that these propositions come because of any irresistible physical magnetism I am exuding. Most of the time, I get the sense that when these men look at me – my hair, my eyes, even my skin – what they really see is not brown and white but blue.

Blue, the color of my passport. Or, rather, the color of both my passports – the Australian *and* the Canadian one.

This sometimes bothers me. And the fact that it bothers me bothers me, too.

My parents spent decades trying to teach me that it's qualities other than beauty that really matter. I'd say I believe that. Why, then, do I catch myself at times like these preferring that someone approach me because he desires me physically than because he desires my citizenship and all the other qualities it represents — escape, freedom, and relative wealth? After all, physical beauty and citizenship are both, to a large extent, assets bestowed on us as accidents of birth. Objectively, citizenship even has some major advantages over beauty — it tends not to depreciate in value over time, and you have to screw up really badly to lose it altogether. Physical assets, however, are subject to degradation caused by any number of things, like gravity, sun damage, neglect, and the overconsumption of ice cream and takeout Chinese food.

"Do you do lots of travel for work?" Gabriel asked me suddenly, interrupting my concentrated study of page 231.

"Yes, lots of travel!" I said, trying to sound busy, mobile, unavailable.

"I travel lots, too, but when I get married I will stay at home with my wife and our children," he said, clearly hoping I would take the hint and apply for a starring role in *that* story line immediately.

My strategy during these conversations is to be reserved but polite. Rarely will I be confrontational and firmly shut someone down. Sometimes, however, I will run away.

I dug for the last of my Ghanaian Cedes and headed for the small stall selling bottled water. Then I wandered into the one store in the airport, thinking.

It's not that I blame the men for trying, I don't. I even admire their moxie sometimes. It's more that I hate the way it makes me feel defensive and objectified when I suspect that I'm simply being seen as a walking one-way ticket to wealth and a better life. But why should I feel any less objectified, or any more flattered, by a man looking for a pretty smile and a tight shirt?

"Perhaps," I thought as I stood alone in the airport on that sultry morning in October, "I've been coming at this all wrong.

Maybe my parents are right. It is other qualities that matter more than beauty – it's my passports. Maybe I should start seeing them as just as tangible (and more indestructible) assets than my cup size."

Behind me a voice called my name.

I turned and looked up. Gabriel had come to find me, to make sure I'd heard that they had called pre-boarding. He pressed a piece of paper containing his phone number and an email address into my hands.

"Where I come from we have a saying" he said, "'My blood met your blood.' When I saw you here today, *my* blood met *your* blood." He looked at me meaningfully and paused.

"Then again," I thought, "maybe I should just invest in a fake wedding ring. Call me demanding, but I need someone to be drawn to my passports, my pretty smile, and my personality."

I smiled, awkward, and tucked the slip of paper into my bag.

"It was nice meeting you, too."

Washington, D.C., USA

TWO MONTHS AFTER TRANSITING through Washington's Dulles Airport on my way home from that trip to Ghana, I was back on the East Coast again to spend Christmas with my family.

Washington D.C. can be a magical place to spend Christmas.

The last time we had all spent Christmas together in D.C., we were living there during my last year of high school. That year we walked out of the candlelit warmth of the Christmas Eve service and into a still, deep cold. Snow was falling straight and thick from an inky void, the flakes so incandescent they seemed a stately, silent parade of displaced stars. The everyday landscape had already disappeared under a transforming layer of white. I can still remember the paradoxically warm tingle of midnight snow on my tongue and how the sudden shock of all that unexpected beauty kindled a reverential hope.

O holy night, indeed.

This Christmas wasn't exactly like that.

We *were* all together. My sister, Michelle, who married her high school love, Jed, was the only one of us still living in D.C., and it was their house we were invading. My parents had come from Australia. So had my brother, Matt, and his girlfriend, Louise. I'd flown over from Los Angeles.

So we were all together, at least. But on Christmas morning it was dripping a cold, dreary rain that did not even bother to pretend that it might turn to snow. And despite the fact that I was wrapped up in a blanket, nursing a cup of coffee and staring at a positive mountain of presents under the Christmas tree, there were no warm tingles, no reverential hope.

Instead there was the feeling that we were all trying hard to create a happy Christmas vibe and not quite getting there. It was Louise's first Christmas away from Australia and she was homesick. Michelle was three months pregnant with her first child and not feeling like eating much, or sitting up. My father was trying too hard to make sure everyone was having a good time, and his anxious organizing was annoying me. Jed, who was periodically calling me by a nickname he knew I loathed, was annoying me, too. And I'm pretty sure we were all annoying Jed, who in that moment was probably feeling a bit sorry that we regularly took his hospitable invitations of "come any time" at face value and descended full force upon his house for two whole weeks instead of just the couple of days that normal American families devote to celebrating the Christmas season.

Collectively we were a bit like an out-of-tune guitar trying to play carols.

This feeling all-out-of-tune thing is aggravating when it

happens after you've worked hard to coordinate travel schedules across continents so that you can spend time together. And it's particularly frustrating when it happens at Christmas, because everyone wants Christmas to be special.

Perhaps that's part of the problem. Christmas *is* a glorious ideal. I love almost everything about it – tiny lights gleaming through a dark and spiky green, the smell of warm sugared cinnamon, the way life slows down and gifts us time with family and friends. I love how the compass of Christmas can point us toward what's truly important in our lives and how the dawning of a new year directs us to consider whether we are living up to our own hopes.

And the music ... How can you hear *O Holy Night* sung with passion and not be stirred?

> *A thrill of hope, the weary world rejoices,*
> *For yonder breaks a new and glorious morn.*
> *Fall on your knees! O, hear the angels' voices!*
> *O night divine...*

There *is* something divine about Christmas – in good years, anyway. But perhaps the very glory of the ideal also risks overburdening the actual day. For if Christmas doesn't quite live up to expectations, you're not just having a below-average day you're having it *on Christmas,* which is ten times worse. It makes you guilty of not only having woken up on the wrong side of the bed but also of transgressing the Ten Commandments of Christmas. For, as we all know, the first of those Ten Commandments is:

Thou shall feel all happy and holy on Christmas morning. Thou shall definitely not *sit on the floor in front of the Christmas tree feeling grumpy and a bit jealous that everyone else has someone to cuddle when all the extra warmth* you *have is a cup of coffee.*

But there I was, guilty as charged and about to be put to the test with regard to another of the Christmas commandments: *Thou shall at all times remember that presents are not the point of Christmas; people are.*

That cold Christmas morning, my little brother was selected as first present-elf. Matt pointed at me, laughed, and pulled eighteen rolls of toilet paper out from where he'd hidden them behind the couch.

"Sorry they're not wrapped," he said.

Considering I'd just been gifted *toilet paper,* it wasn't exactly the lack of wrapping that bothered me.

"They're a stand-in present," Matt said. "Something else is coming, but it didn't get here in time. And, you know, you didn't actually *have* any toilet paper in the house when Lou and I stayed with you."

He had a point. When Matt and Louise had stopped in L.A. for a visit ten days earlier, I'd been out of toilet paper and, thanks to long days at work, remained so for three days.

"Paper towel works just fine if you rip it up into small enough pieces," I said, repeating the argument I had used then.

Lou laughed.

"No," Matt replied, smirking, "paper towel does *not* work just fine."

When my turn came around again, my parents were next. The package they handed me was soft. I opened it to find a T-shirt from my favorite clothes store in Australia. There was only one problem: it was huge.

"This is an extra large," I said, confused, after I checked the tag.

"I *told* you she wasn't an extra large, Merrilyn," Dad said.

"Oh?" Mum said. "I just thought that looked about the right size."

I held the shirt up against me. It came halfway to my knees.

"What size do you normally wear?" Mum asked.

"*Medium!*" I said.

"*Really*?!?" Mum said, "I would have thought you were at least a large."

"Merrilyn!" my father hissed, kicking her.

I was zero for two, but my sister was next. Michelle is very thoughtful and often keeps an eye out for ways to put people at ease, so it's perhaps understandable that I failed to take due notice of the grin she wore – one part naughty, one part proud – as she handed me her present. But even if I'd recognized it as such, I'm pretty sure I still wouldn't have been able to figure out what my younger, married, pregnant sister had wrapped for me so gaily.

It was a book. *The complete book of international adoption: A step-by-step guide to finding your child.*

"What?" Michelle said into the stunned silence that preceded laughter all around the family circle. "You've always said that if you don't get married you'll think about adopting kids. Now you know where to start. And it was on sale for five bucks!"

Los Angeles, USA

I LAUGHED IN THAT moment on Christmas morning. The funny factor outweighed the sting I felt, sitting there in my flannel pajamas, looking around at everyone else neatly paired up with someone. But by April, when my early-morning phone alarm reminded me of my July wedding in Australia, it was getting less funny. I was beginning to worry that Michelle's Christmas present had set the theme for the entire year, for just a week earlier I had also been blindsided by the solitary present I had to open on the morning of my thirty-first birthday.

My birthday started early. Sadly, this was not because of excitement related to piñatas, upcoming parties, or trick candles adorning strawberry cheesecake. It was because I had to drive a friend to the airport at 5 a.m. after a weekend spent celebrating Robin's long-awaited wedding.

I hadn't planned anything to mark this birthday – I'd known my California crowd would be all partied out after spending most of the weekend at various wedding-related events. So I had fully intended to get up early, do the airport run, and come back and get straight to work on the final draft of my first novel. I'd already been working on rewriting the novel for a year, and the final copy-editing deadlines were looming. But when I got back from the airport at 6:30 a.m. that Sunday and looked between my desk and my pillow, it wasn't even a close call.

I was so going back to sleep.

As I climbed back into bed I ripped open the padded yellow envelope that had arrived four days earlier adorned with stern instructions that it was to be saved until my birthday.

Inside that envelope was another book, posted to me by one of my best friends from Australia, Tash.

The title of *this* book was *Spinsters Abroad: Victorian Lady Explorers*. On the cover was a small brunette. She was wearing a white lacy dress buttoned to her chin and a pith helmet. She was shading this unlikely ensemble with a parasol and stepping daintily through the jungle.

"What spurred so many Victorian women to leave behind their secure middle-class homes and undertake perilous journeys of thousands of miles, tramping through tropical forests, caravanning across deserts, and scaling mountain ranges?" asked the back cover. "And how were they able to travel so freely in exotic lands, when at home such independence was denied to them?"

This scintillating manifesto on international singleness was still lying on my bedside table five days later when my phone woke me with its shrill commands to get engaged, and while I wasn't amused that morning, by dinner that night I'd regained some of my sense of humor.

"I want to write an essay about this whole topic of being single at thirty-one," I explained to my flatmate, Travis, from where I was sitting on a stool behind the kitchen counter while he made both of us dinner. "But I don't want people to wonder whether I'm just putting a brave face on acute psychic pain."

"They won't. They'll just think you're being a drama queen, as usual," Travis reassured me. "But while we're on the topic, *are* you putting a brave face on acute psychic pain? I mean, I'm thirty and single and I'm just fine with that. But I think this whole topic is harder for women. There seems to be something about turning thirty that freaks women out. And, let's face it, I can still have children when I'm seventy if I want to. You can't.""

MY FIRST INSTINCT WAS to issue a quick and emphatic denial in response to Travis' question about pain.

Sure, being single at thirty-one was not exactly how I had imagined my life playing out when I was in high school. When I was fifteen I had this all sorted. I wouldn't get married at twenty-one as my parents had. Instead, I'd leave it daringly late and marry at twenty-four. I'd have my first baby at twenty-seven. And I would somehow manage to do all this while being a trauma surgeon and living in Africa.

According to that plan, I am now both off-track and way behind schedule.

But there have been some very good things about my teenage plans' being turned on their head. If I had married at twenty-four – just after finishing six years of study to qualify as a forensic psychologist – I would not have been free to ring up my parents, confess that I wasn't that keen anymore on working as a psychologist and ask whether I could come live with them for a while and try my hand at writing novels while I looked for jobs in the humanitarian field.

When one such job opportunity arose, I probably would not have been able to take off on twelve days' notice to move to Croatia.

After living for a while in the Balkans, I might not have been able to accept a scholarship to spend a year doing another master's degree in peace studies just because it sounded like fun. Or relocate to California afterward simply because it seemed like a good idea to take a job in Los Angeles as a stress-management trainer for humanitarian workers – a job that keeps me traveling at least one week out of four and sometimes for weeks on end.

I may never have finished my first novel, which I wrote on weekends, when I was beholden to no one but myself.

I would not have had nearly as much time to invest in a wide, rich friendship network that encircles the globe.

All of this I knew, but there was no denying that there *had* been something about turning thirty that was profoundly unsettling.

RIGHT UP UNTIL I was 29 years 8 months and 14 days old, I thought turning thirty was no big deal. Then I noticed I was preempting *the* question.

You know, *that* question.

"How are you feeling about the big three-0?"

I'd started answering this question before the other person had even finished asking. I'd pull a bland adjective out of thin air

– *fine, good, great* – and deliver it with breezy unconcern.

Then I'd let it sit there.

The other person would usually pause, waiting for me to fill the silence with bright protestations about how I *really was* fine with the fact that I was turning thirty and still single, with no prospects of popping out babies any time soon, and how it's all been worth it because I love my job and I wouldn't trade all the experiences I've had in the past ten years for anything. All this was true, but I didn't like being expected to say it. And when I didn't oblige with the culturally correct dialogue, the conversation usually moved on.

The day I turned 29 years 8 months and 14 days old, however, the conversation didn't move on. I looked up to notice that the person who had just asked me *the* question was staring at me with rather more puzzlement than I thought the answer warranted.

"What?" I said.

"*Fine?*" she repeated.

"Uh-huh."

"I ask you how you're feeling about the situation in Somalia and all you have to say is *fine?*" she said.

Oh.

This was when I started to get annoyed. I didn't want to be one of those people who have a crisis about turning thirty. Even now, a year later, I still can't figure out exactly what might be unsettling me, given that I don't think the ticking of my biological clock is anywhere near becoming an imperative.

I know it's possible that I am subconsciously worried about this inexorable biological countdown, but despite offhand comments to family and friends about how I plan to adopt kids if I never get married, I really don't think it's my major concern.

When I look at other people's children, no matter how cute, I still mostly just feel relieved that they're not mine. This was only underscored by a conversation I had recently with my boss's wife.

"Oh, little Sam's getting over his first bad cold," she said, exhausted, when I asked her how the kids were. "He's not really sick anymore, just miserable. He's been hanging off my leg, whining, wanting to be held all the time, and I can't get anything done."

"Gee," I said, "that must make you want to bend down and tell him, 'Get used to it, buddy, that's life. You're going to feel crappy sometimes and people can't put everything on hold to pay attention to you every time you're grumpy. Deal with it.'"

"Ummm, no," she said, clearly making a mental note never to ask me to baby-sit. "It makes me want to pick him up and comfort him."

No, I don't feel ready for kids yet. I don't have that powerful soul-deep hunger to be a mother that I hear some of my girlfriends talk about. I'm not sure I ever will. But I *am* starting to catch myself wondering sometimes, in a much more abstract fashion, whether I'm going to miss out altogether on those beauties and struggles peculiar to parenthood or on learning how to be genuinely vulnerable in a way I suspect that only the bond of marriage allows. And whether, if I do, I'll wake up in fifteen years and still believe that it was worth it – this choice that I have made again and again throughout my twenties to pursue adventure and novelty and helping people in faraway lands rather than stability and continuity and helping people in a land I claim as mine.

These are melancholy moments. These are days when I wake up and wonder whether I wouldn't perhaps feel happier, more fulfilled or less restless on a radically different path. When I would really like to come home to someone who's vowed to be interested in how my day was. When I just want someone to bring me coffee in bed or rub my shoulders uninvited.

Yet, right alongside these wonderings that sometimes dead-end in visions of my dying alone at ninety lie other wonderings, other fears.

After a nomadic life that has been largely defined by coming and (always, inevitably) going, am I even capable of the sort of commitment demanded by marriage and children and a place called home?

I touched on this confused tangle of longings recently with a girlfriend for whom I was a bridesmaid a decade ago. Jane is now living on a verdant pecan farm in Australia ten miles from my parents' place, complete with a sweet prince of a husband, two little girls, a dog, two cats, a horse, and a veggie garden.

"You know, I want your life sometimes," I confessed near the end of our conversation.

Jane laughed. "My brain is turning to mush with no one but the kids to talk to all day, and when you say that you spent – Eloise, I told you to stay at the table while you finished your milk! Sit back down please – when you say that you spent last week in Boston at a conference and you're off to New York next week, *I* want *your* life."

"NO," I SAID TO Travis in our kitchen in Los Angeles that night after thinking for a minute or two about his question. "I don't often put a brave face on acute pain. I'm happy by myself. Mostly. It's just that sometimes I wonder about a different life, you know?"

"Yeah," Travis said, doubtless wondering whether he would ever achieve his dream of making it big as a Hollywood director and be able to quit his day job. "I know all about that. Write about that."

Los Angeles – Accra – Washington, D.C. – **Sydney – Zagreb – South Bend – Nairobi – San Diego** – Atlanta – Madang – Kona – Canberra – London – Baltimore – Itonga – Vancouver – Harare – Dushanbe – Lira – Petats – Port Moresby – Brisbane – Ballina – Malibu

ALTERNATE LIVES

Los Angeles, USA

WHEN IT COMES TO wondering about a different life, mine is not my parents' story. Both of them grew up firmly planted on farms in Australia. My father milked cows before and after school, wore hand-me-down clothes, and still talks with emotion of the treat that it was to have roast chicken on Christmas Day. My mother attended the two-room schoolhouse just down the road from their sugar cane farm. Hers was a childhood full of chores, too, but also of fishing in the river across the road and caravanning at the nearby beach every summer. When my parents decided to attend university, they were treading a different path from most of their peers. They were also leaving the only homes they had ever known.

After a childhood of unfathomable stability, marriage to each

other at twenty-one, and seven years spent living in Canberra (a
strong contender for the planet's most boring capital city), I can
understand why my parents wondered about a different life. I can
understand the allure of a radical new path. I can understand –
though still I marvel at their naïve bravery – why they decided
to pack up their three young children and move to Bangladesh to
pursue development work.

My grandparents were less understanding. My mother's
parents even suggested that if they *must* go, we children should
stay with them.

"Don't worry," my parents reassured them. "It's only for two
years. Then we'll be back."

Twenty-one years and seven international moves later, my
parents finally relocated back to Australia. During their time
away, they'd weathered two government coups and several
emergency evacuations and collected more than their share of
interesting experiences. They'd also raised three global nomads
who were equally accustomed to spending time in seaside resorts
and slums and who felt one part self-assured citizens of the
world and two parts outsiders pretty much wherever they went.

This is why I still don't fully understand my own perpetual
wonderings about a different life – I have already had many lives
in many places. And the life I now live is the sort of life that my
parents left Australia hoping to find in Bangladesh.

I am the director of education and training services for a
nonprofit organization dedicated to providing psychological
support services to humanitarian workers around the world.
When I am not delivering workshops on stress, trauma, and
resilience in cities as divergent as Amsterdam or Nairobi, I
find myself in Los Angeles. To outside observers interested in
this sort of work, I look as if I have it made – a meaningful job
with frequent travel and a home base in one of the great cities

of the developed world. And when I come across these outside observers, often students who are longing to find an entrée into humanitarian work, they all want to know pretty much the same thing.

How did you get your job? How did you get your life?

These, I am afraid, are entirely valid questions without satisfying answers. I often feel as if these students are looking for a set of instructions they can use to map out a clear pathway for themselves. What they get instead, if I'm being honest, is a shrug. For the truth of the matter is, I'm still not entirely sure *how* I got this job, much less this life that can still feel as if it doesn't fit me quite right.

Sydney, Australia

WHEN I HAVE THE time to give someone the extended version of the pathway to now, I usually begin the story in Sydney, around the time I graduated with a master's degree in forensic psychology. By this time, after six years of learning to call Australia home and actually mean it, I had figured out that a large part of my heart was still overseas and that I wanted to be an international humanitarian worker.

At least that's how I put it to my parents when I rang them where they were living at the time to let them know that now that I'd invested all this effort and no small sum of their money into psychology, I wasn't sure I wanted to be a psychologist anymore.

"Why not?" Mum asked reasonably.

"I just feel like I really *should* be overseas," I said, stopping just short of claiming divine directive on the topic, "and I don't want to work in prison again."

I knew Mum wouldn't argue with that second point. My parents hadn't been thrilled when I announced my decision to specialize in forensics. Neither were they charmed upon learning that my first internship would have me spending six months in the maximum-security unit of Australia's largest prison for men, and I doubt that my subsequent anecdotes about making knives out of toothbrushes and smuggling drugs in tennis balls did all that much to reassure them. They were much happier when I left the prison and moved on to my next rotation, with the state police. Or, at least, they were happy until they found out the types of cases we were regularly called in for: child abuse, sexual assault, shootings, and particularly nasty homicides.

"So can I come stay with you in the Philippines for a while?" I asked.

Mum sighed over the long-distance line.

"I knew you should have done organizational psychology," she said.

"*Mum*," I said. "Organizational psychology is boring."

"It's *not* boring," she said in a familiar refrain. "It's what I would have done if I'd studied psychology."

"And you would have been very good at it," I said, "seeing as how you're naturally equipped for the post of benevolent dictator of a small country. But I am not you, and *I* think it's boring."

"You think everything not extreme, dark, or dangerous is boring," my mother replied calmly. "I don't understand *where* you got that from. Certainly not from your father or me."

"I *could* just get a job in Australia," I said, playing my trump card. "Probably the only ones left in my field now are back in maximum security or in the sex offenders unit. Or maybe I can stay with the police."

"Okay, stop it," Mum said. "You can come and stay with us for a while. But what are you planning on actually *doing*?"

Much as she clearly loves us, no one has ever accused my

mother of suffering from empty-nest syndrome. On the contrary, I think she threw a party the day all three of us were finally out of the house.

"I'm going to write a novel," I said. "And volunteer with nonprofits and look for a job with a humanitarian organization."

In response to this, I now realize, my parents would have been perfectly within their rights to say, "Um, hello? We just put you through six years of higher education so you could *leave* your developed-world haven? Instead of getting a paying job, you want to move back in with us, volunteer in the slums, search out ways to relocate to Africa, and write a novel? *Write a novel?* What are you *thinking?* You don't know anything about writing novels!"

But they didn't say that.

They said okay.

And I packed my bags for Manila.

Zagreb, Croatia

I SPENT FIVE MONTHS in the Philippines trying to write my novel and working as a volunteer before I got my first job offer. The offer was for a professional internship in the Balkans, but not as a human rights advocate or an election monitor or any one of a dozen other roles I had thought I might fall into. Instead, the development organization that was interested in my resume seemed to actually *want* the psychology training I was so willing to leave behind, and I ended up in Croatia providing trauma-counseling and stress-management training to its staff.

After six months of this, I knew two things: that my heart really *was* in humanitarian work and that I could do with some more training if I wanted to work as anything but a trauma specialist.

Don't get me wrong – I think trauma psychologists do amazing and necessary work. I just didn't think I was a particularly *good* one. I'd picked forensics in the first place largely because it sounded mysterious and sexy. But it stops being a game very quickly when you're trying to talk someone out of killing himself. Or when you're standing in the emergency room beside someone who has just been in an accident and may never walk again. Or sitting with someone still covered in soot and ash who has tried and failed to save a baby from a burning car.

In choosing forensics, I hadn't quite realized I was signing up to be the keeper of people's worst moments, fears, and impulses. I'd gotten more than I bargained for, and way more than I felt equipped to deal with capably at twenty-five.

I knew that I *did* want to help people who desperately needed it, but I also wanted to do it in a way that wouldn't so often leave me feeling completely out of my depth – simultaneously helpless and responsible for having some answers. So at the end of my six months in Croatia, in a second attempt to abandon the minefields of extreme emotion, I decided to return to school and pick up another degree that might better qualify me to work in actual minefields instead.

Sydney, Australia

VERY OCCASIONALLY THERE ARE moments in life when you can actually *see* a door swing open in front of you and everything changes in an instant. Reading the email that informed me that I'd been accepted to Notre Dame University's master's program in international peace studies was one of those moments.

I was back in Sydney after my time in Croatia, working

as a researcher on a child death review team. I was sipping a midmorning latte and reviewing a particularly terrible case when I heard the little chime announcing incoming email. I had to read it at least twice before I took it in.

Along with twenty-one other candidates from eighteen countries, I'd been awarded a full scholarship and a stipend to cover living expenses. The program started in four months – could I be in Indiana by then?

I thought this master's program would be a fantastically interesting way to spend a year. I also thought it would open doors to jobs that were more traditionally humanitarian work. If I'd had to guess, that morning that found me peering through an open door at Notre Dame's famous golden dome, I would have said I'd spend a year there and then move back to Africa.

I'd have been wrong.

South Bend, USA

IN MANY WAYS, THE course I would follow after leaving Notre Dame was set during only my second weekend in Indiana.

Over in the Philippines, my parents had figured out that I would be living just twenty minutes from friends they'd met years earlier in Indonesia. Mum and Dad rang me, very excited, to tell me that these friends, Wyn and Carol, had offered to be my in-country surrogate parents – starting with picking me up and taking me to church that weekend.

"Thanks," I told them. "Just to remind you, I am now twenty-six years old and perhaps a little past surrogate parents. But thanks."

I went, of course. My parents had been so thrilled to put the pieces together, and after the intensity of orientation week, getting out of the apartments was appealing. And the novel I was (still) working on was set in Ambon. Wyn and Carol had lived there for twelve years during their time in Indonesia. They were bound to be gold mines of information about this place I'd never visited.

On the way to church that Sunday, Wyn asked what I'd been doing in Croatia that had led me to Notre Dame.

"Huh," he said when I was done explaining. "My brother-in-law has just set up an organization in California that helps humanitarian workers with stress and trauma. You should really talk to him."

No way, I thought, smiling and nodding. I'd come to Notre Dame to move away from that!

But Wyn saw something and didn't let it go. He introduced me via email to the president of the Headington Institute, and when I didn't follow up he rang his brother-in-law and badgered him into contacting me himself.

"You've got a great background for this work," my future boss told me when we finally connected by phone.

"Yeah," I said, "but I'm really not sure if I want to work with stress and trauma again. And I won't be done with this master's for another eight months."

"Why don't you think about it for a while?" he said. "I'm a patient man."

In the end, it was my classmates at Notre Dame who tipped the scales toward taking the job at the Headington Institute. Well, them and the fact that all other doors I tried to push on remained stubbornly shut.

Someone I loved very much that year – loved in ways I often thought would break me – shared his private nightmares of Bosnia, Rwanda, and East Timor. But there were other classmates who talked openly that year, too. They told stories of war and loss, depression and loneliness, damaging collisions with new cultures, and their drive to create positive change in the face of it all.

There was not a lot to do at night where we lived besides sit around together in one of the apartments in the complex we all shared, curled up on ratty old couches, drinking wine, telling stories, and chewing on similar questions over and over again.

What drove us toward this work and kept us going?

What was it granting us, costing, and changing?

At this particular point in my own journey, I felt acutely lonely and more adrift than ever. But as I listened to my classmates talk of their own turmoil, hungry for answers and metaphors and safe places to store their experiences, I started to wonder whether this might be my niche after all. And whether, if I could learn more about how to help people grapple with their own inner turbulence, I might also find some tools for tackling mine.

I would go to Los Angeles for two years, I decided. If at the end of that time I didn't feel as if my work with the institute was worthwhile, I'd leave. I'd pursue human rights in Africa. Again.

Nairobi, Kenya

EIGHT MONTHS AFTER STARTING my new job, I found myself kneeling on the cold cement floor of a dormitory bathroom in Nairobi. I blinked the sweat out of my eyes and tried to read my watch. It was hard to focus. Three hours since I had started throwing up. I'd given up trying to figure out whether it was malaria or plain old food poisoning. By 3 a.m. I was past that. I was just sure that whatever it was, I'd be dead by dawn.

I was not dead by dawn, something I did not feel well enough to celebrate with anything but a trace of disappointed resignation. At 6:30 on a chilly Kenyan morning, I faced the fact that it was probably food poisoning, that I would probably live, and that in exactly two hours I was scheduled to be standing in front of twenty humanitarian workers from all over Africa, teaching about providing peer support after trauma.

The first three days of this four-day training that I was facilitating had been … character-building. *Character-building*, as usual, being code for *experiences that suck so much while you're going through them that the most effective solace available is the firm belief in future noble and virtuous personal benefits*. One good thing, though, was the location. Back in Africa for the first time in eleven years, I'd recognized the shape of the trees, flat against the horizon. The red dirt, the taste of warm Sprite from a dusty glass bottle, dark clouds of pollution billowing from every second vehicle, the awareness that I was a walking dollar sign – all were familiar from spending my teenage years in Zimbabwe.

What was not so familiar was the role I now wore like an uncomfortable suit, that of an expert in stress and trauma management. Coming from Australia with all its insistence on uniformly sized poppies, being proclaimed an expert in anything never sits well. And I was finding the ironies inherent in being a supposed expert in this particular field at the ripe old age of twenty-eight difficult to ignore. But as soon as I stepped into my role with the institute, I began to relearn that important lesson I first grasped at sixteen when we moved back to the United States and I convinced my entire class that in Zimbabwe we'd occasionally ridden elephants to school and summered in a giant treehouse: Other people will believe almost anything if you say it with enough confidence and conviction. It's just that I had always thought that being a "grown-up" would mean actually *feeling* that confidence. By the time I landed in Kenya, I was starting to think it just meant being better at pretending.

"At least," I consoled myself, "I must be getting better at the pretending."

Moses, one of the participants from Kenya, stopped me as I locked up the conference room one night. "Can you ever turn it off, the psychology, when you're with your friends?" he wanted to know. "Or do you think like that all the time?" I knew what he was asking. During the past couple of years, I've encountered this over and over at dinner parties, in airplanes, basically any time I introduce myself and explain what I do. It usually boils down to one basic question: Can you read my mind? And one basic fear: Can you see my secret shame?

My standard response is to tell people that my psychology specialty is forensics, so unless they have criminal tendencies they're safe from my powers. When I really want to freak someone out, I'll pause after that piece of lighthearted banter, narrow my eyes and look at them speculatively. Moses, however, was without guile, and I didn't have the heart to try that on him.

I paused, searching for a way to reassure him that his innermost thoughts were safer than he could imagine without making me sound *completely* clueless. He didn't wait for my answer, though.

"I think it must be very uncomfortable to be around you," the 6-foot-3, muscle-bound giant said, beaming at me without malice, white teeth flashing.

I walked away from him ten minutes later both flattered and disturbed. Flattered because someone, at least, thought I had some answers. To life. Disturbed because someone thought I had some answers. To life.

This first trip to Kenya for work threw this paradox into sharp relief for me. It was my job, I suddenly realized, to understand how difficult, how dangerous and how incredibly enriching international humanitarian work can prove. It was my job to convince humanitarian workers that unless they consistently pay attention to caring for themselves while they're working to care for others, they will be lucky to last for three years before returning home spent, disillusioned and possibly traumatized. It was my job to know that about a quarter of humanitarians working outside the developed world can expect to undergo a life-threatening experience during their assignment. And it was my job to know what could help when these most horrendous events – the carjackings, kidnappings, land mines, shootings and tsunamis of life – blindside us on a pedestrian Tuesday afternoon.

On one level, I knew, I could do this. I had already lived in eight countries and traveled in many more. A passion for international humanitarian work was born the year my family moved to Bangladesh and I asked, with the innocence of a sheltered seven-year-old, whether God had run out of money halfway around the world. I had found that I could help people discover what self-care strategies might help sustain them in the face of the loneliness that can come with being far from family, the weariness that attends constant exposure to disaster, and the mental pressure of making decisions that mean some people receive lifesaving aid while others do not.

Most of it is not rocket science. Even now I sometimes feel ridiculous facing some of the most dedicated and passionate individuals I have ever met and advising them that drinking too much is not an incredibly helpful self-care strategy and that they might want to consider journaling instead. But this is the sort of message humanitarian workers need to hear on a regular basis. Most start out in this field young, idealistic and vulnerable. When they find themselves working in an understaffed and undersupplied refugee camp facing more desperate people than they can possibly hope to help, it doesn't take long before far too many take refuge themselves in alcohol, risk-taking, casual sex or cynicism in an effort to cope.

On a personal level, however, I found myself during this first trip back to Africa wanting more, much more. What I really wanted to know was why. Why was there so much suffering in this world? Why did humans have such a talent for violence? How did I reconcile the divine omnipotence I was taught to trust in as a child with the pain and incomprehension of those whose lives had been torn apart by an earthquake, a famine, a tsunami, or other people? If God existed, if he were paying attention, why did he often seem so slow to act and so silent? And why had I been given so much while others had so little?

But while I wanted the answers to these questions of meaning, they were the very answers I was most keenly aware that I did not have. Not in the way that would ever let me start a sentence with the word *because* and feel any degree of certainty in the answer.

I consoled myself by remembering that most people I knew who believed that they had "those answers" were far more annoying than inspiring or comforting.

Perhaps, I thought, it was more about understanding the questions that are raised than knowing "the answers."

Perhaps, I thought, one of these days I would say that and it wouldn't feel like a cop-out.

Los Angeles, USA

MY STANDARD LINE WHEN I arrived in L.A. was that I expected to be there about two years. In all honesty, this mantra came about more because I was unable to visualize anything concrete beyond a two-year horizon than because of any well-thought-out life plan. In fact, whenever anyone asks me where I see myself in five years, the first word that always pops into my head is *Nigeria*.

I have no idea why. I have never been to Nigeria and had no particular yen to move there. Perhaps it is just shorthand for "So far in life I've moved internationally twelve times. Five years ago I could never have predicted I would end up in L.A. working with humanitarian workers. I couldn't have controlled that process if I tried, yet it's felt right. You *really* expect me to know where life will have taken me five years from now?"

Some might say this attitude denotes a certain degree of emotional instability, core identity issues, and a pathological need to keep my options open.

Some might say it indicates adaptability, zest for life, a high tolerance for ambiguity, and a realistic view of how much control we have over the future.

Some might even say that it demonstrates a commendable willingness to stay open to divine guidance down the path of life and a remarkable spiritual maturity.

Whatever it *actually* indicates, I blame it (as so many other things) in large part on my parents. *They* left for what they assured *their* parents would be two years, too. This was why, of all people to take my two-year mantra seriously, four years into my tenure in Los Angeles I was surprised by certain signs that they were doing exactly that.

My mother may never hesitate to remind me that my own mental health (not to mention my bank balance) would have been better served by my pursuing a different branch of psychology, but to their credit, my parents have never lodged serious objections to my global meanderings. I know they probably worry sometimes, but the worst I've gotten over the years from Mum is a diffident "Well, it'd be good if you *didn't* have to go to Haiti next week."

But as I entered my fifth year in Los Angeles, I began to notice a subtle shift in her tactics.

The previous May, six months after my parents had finally moved back to Australia, my siblings and I had converged on their place for what we hoped would be a relaxing week. The morning after we arrived, however, the three of us trailed dutifully out to the shed to engage in the parental-mandated activity of packing and unpacking boxes, also known as "organizing our stuff."

Organizing our stuff means braving snakes, spiders, and rats in the back shed to unpack some of the many boxes containing fragments of our mobile childhood, provide a compelling argument as to why Mum should not be allowed to put said fragments in the "throw away" pile, and repacking it all and labeling it so that we will be able do this all over again even more efficiently in another two years. Organizing our stuff does not rank highly on any McKay child's list of "favorite things to do on holiday".

This time, though, it was proving more tolerable than usual. My sister unearthed a stack of stories she'd written in her first-grade class in Bangladesh, and I was immensely gratified to see that they all featured me as the main character or at least the driving force in the story plot. I was flicking through my own first-grade stories, happily basking in the warm glow cast by decades-old sibling worship, when Mum dropped the bombshell.

"The Salvation Army truck is coming next week, and we thought we'd just load this on with everything else."

The "this" she was indicating so casually was the first and only decent piece of furniture I'd ever bought on Australian soil, a pine dresser. I was very attached to this dresser. When I bought it I was still in graduate school and it had represented a huge step for me. It was brand new, it cost me $300, and there was no way

I could fit it in a suitcase. That dresser represented stability and belonging and sinking my emotional roots deep into the rich red soil of my home country. It had helped cement my Australian identity. So what if it had now been sitting in storage ever since I had left Australia seven years earlier for what I'd said would be two years?

"I want to keep it," I said. "I'll need it when I come home in two years."

"Okay," Dad said. "We weren't going to tell you this, but a family of mice chewed through the back and made a nest in there and peed all over everything."

Great. My Australian identity was now saturated with mouse piss.

"Fine then," I sulked. "Give it away."

"We'll help you buy other stuff when you come home," Mum wheedled. "Nice stuff."

That was the start of the uncharacteristically maternal offers that have recently been linked to the words *come home*.

Dad is typically the soft touch in our family. He is prone to excessive guilt regarding any issue remotely related to inherited physical challenges or to emotional scarring that may have been caused by our peripatetic upbringing. This makes him good for all sorts of things from prescription glasses, to phone cards that facilitate our staying connected to friends worldwide, to family-funded credit cards to be used in case of an emergency, to sneakers.

Come to think of it, I'm not exactly sure *why* he continues to buy all of us sneakers at regular intervals, but it's very nice of him.

Mum is more pragmatic and less indulgent. She says that none of us would trade our childhood international experiences no matter what they have cost us and suggests that since we are all now past our mid-twenties, perhaps it's time we kids started buying our own expensive sneakers.

This is why I was surprised when it was Mum who began casually dropping the phrase *come home* into conversations. If I came home, she said, she'd help me look for another job and buy me furniture and fly me up to Ballina for the odd holiday.

I wasn't using all that psychology education to counsel, but I hadn't forgotten my thorough grounding in trend analysis. I figured that it was only a matter of time before the stakes in the "come home" campaign escalated, but nothing had prepared me for what she flippantly said one night, right in the middle of a completely unrelated discussion.

"If you came home," Mum said, "we could get you the house across the road. It's for sale. It's got forty acres, two waterfalls and a spectacular view. It's a writer's paradise, and you could walk over and have breakfast with us."

"How much is it?" I asked.

"$770,000," Mum said.

There was awed silence. I think even Dad was taken aback.

"Pocket change," I said.

Dad snorted.

"What else?" I asked, teasing back. "I'm getting out of bed to get a pen and I'm writing this down so that I can consider the offer carefully tomorrow."

"Well, I don't know if I'd call it an *offer* exactly," Mum said, backpedaling.

"You clearly said, 'We could get you,'" I said.

"That's right," Dad said, joining in on the fun. "I was a little surprised, but that *is* what you said."

"Fine," Mum said, clearly figuring that if she was in for a penny she may as well be in for $770,000 plus some extras. "What else? There are stables. I'll throw in a couple of horses."

"It sounds perfect." I said. "I think you should buy it now. That way it'll be there for me when I come home in two years."

San Diego, USA

THE THING IS, ALMOST six months after my thirty-first birthday, more than four years after I moved to L.A., I was surprised to find that my two-year timeline had shifted with me. When asked, I was still saying I could see myself staying here "about two more years." Yet I was also still tempted to abandon current realities and follow the lure of the unknown toward possibility and trust that little voice that whispered to me of greener pastures elsewhere, of love that surely must be waiting just across the next ocean, of happier alternate lives.

One Saturday morning I talked this over with two of my closest friends in California, Erica and Leah.

If you had seen the three of us that morning sipping lattes around a small table adorned with blue and yellow print, eyeing the pastries while the trams rattled past, you might have thought we were in Fontainebleau or Melbourne. Either would have been a good guess. The dark-eyed waiter spoke with a French accent. All three of us spoke with Australian ones. Not much about the scene spelled San Diego, but that's where we were.

Two traveling husbands spelled girls weekend away. And girls weekend away spelled breakfast out. And while you might have thought a Saturday breakfast would spell sleepy chatter about our families, our men, or our plans for the day, it didn't. It meant focusing on the one topic we all needed to debrief before we could wander along the marina or through Little Italy or into the lingerie store (where I would later dust myself and whoever was standing nearby with body glitter and then find the scented candles and wonder how I could go about getting paid to come up with advertising phrases like "The spicy allure of warm blackberries suggests languid summer love in the grass").

No, before the marina and Little Italy, and definitely before body glitter and languid summer love in the grass, we needed to talk work.

This took a while.

Leah is a composer. She was finishing up a year as a Fulbright scholar, negotiating a music licensing contract in the states, and discussing projects on the home front with her Australian agent.

Erica is a scientist at UCLA's Cousins Center for Psychoneuroimmunology. She focuses on cancer and stress, and since her field is so specialized that it doesn't exist in my spell-checker, I'm not sure why I'm still surprised when Erica says things like "Next week I really need to order the primers of metastasis-related genes to test timing effects of nadolol," and I really don't have a clue what she's talking about.

When it was my turn to update the others on the last week, I led off with "I'm in the middle of launching a global program called CARD – Counselors Assisting Relief and Development – to register mental health professionals worldwide who are interested in working with humanitarian workers." Then I sighed and told the whole truth. "It might sound glamorous, but it mostly comes down to a lot of emailing."

I thought about the previous week and sighed again.

At times my job could certainly bring adventure, but what I didn't talk about nearly as often were the weeks when I did little more than write emails. Emails to the keynote speakers for the symposium I was organizing in Baltimore. Emails to the Kenya program trying to get them to confirm workshop dates for October. Emails to the Ghana program seeking same. And, that week, an endless stream of emails to publicize the existence of

CARD.

Erica and Leah would have cheerfully listened to me describe what spending the week sending emails had been like. They would have asked intelligent questions about the programs and how I was structuring my day to help me stay focused and motivated. But it was Saturday morning. Suddenly I didn't want to whine about emails. Suddenly I didn't even want to *think* about emails.

"What would you do if you weren't doing what you're doing?" I asked them instead. "I mean, if you were living an alternate life, what would you do?"

I don't know what I expected them to say, but it certainly wasn't something quite so sensible.

"Maybe I'd teach," Leah said.

"I could be a consultant," Erica said. "No more lab coats. Bring on suits and high heels. What about you?"

"I'd own a pizza shop in Ballina near Mum's and Dad's place," I said.

Erica and Leah did not laugh. They did, however, look at me in a way that made it clear they weren't sure whether I was serious or joking and would suspend all judgment until they figured that out.

"Okay, not a pizza shop, exactly," I said. "An Italian restaurant with white linen tablecloths, a wood-fired oven, and tall candles lodged in wine bottles. The scent of fresh garlic bread would season the air while my customers dined on homemade pumpkin ravioli in a sage and brown butter sauce."

I was making myself hungry, no small feat considering I had just polished off two crepes slathered in nutella. I wondered if it would be bad form to lick out the nutella pot. Probably. I swiped the edge of it with my finger and licked that instead.

I think about alternate lives a lot. Growing up, I spent days on end pretending I was an orphaned English child being raised as a Hindu Indian Princess, a child who would eventually be rescued by a dashing British soldier after the aged (and impotent) bridegroom whom I had been forced to wed at the age of thirteen suddenly died and I was expected to follow custom and immolate myself on his funeral pyre.

This is another one I blame on my parents. They're the ones who gave me the thousand-page novel *The Far Pavilions* to read when I was nine.

At thirty-one, however, my fantasy selves tended to live in two rather divergent worlds. Down one path lay khaki pants, orphanages, and refugee camps in Africa. Down the other lay fresh pasta and an Italian restaurant in a small sugar-cane farming town in Australia, a place where I could eventually get to know half of the people in town, where making bread dough would substitute for hours on a computer, and where the saddest stories I'd hear would usually be on the evening news.

I am fully aware that by living in L.A. and working with a nonprofit, I am daily living out other people's alternate-life fantasies. But that doesn't negate the fact that the basic economic principle of opportunity cost holds just as true in relation to the wealth of time as it does for money. By choosing this, I am giving up other lives – different lives that would shape a different me.

Some of those alternate lives are easy to pass up. I mean, who in her right mind would really risk being burned alive on the funeral pyre of her deceased husband in India? However, some aren't so easy to pass up. Not living in a small country town (regardless of whether my mother is right and I'd go stir crazy in six months) is costing me a whole different set of experiences, relationships, and life lessons.

Robert Frost took the road less traveled and it made all the difference for him, but even if he'd choose it again without hesitating, I'd wager he wondered about that other path occasionally.

As we spent four hours crawling up the freeway on Sunday afternoon on our way back to L.A., Erica and I had plenty of time to wistfully contemplate other paths, paths free of millions of other cars carrying people who'd apparently also gotten the idea that San Diego was the place to go that weekend. Roads way less traveled had rarely looked so good, and Erica circled back around to this topic.

"What keeps us doing what we're doing then?" Erica asked. "Because all three of us could live those alternate lives."

She was right. Leah could teach, Erica could consult, and I could own a restaurant. Those two, at least, would be very good at their alter-lives. So what kept Leah scoring music, Erica separating cells, and me writing emails during weeks or even months when it just wasn't much fun? What made us choose this path and stick to it for years?

What drives any of us to stick with something for years when it's not a constant carnival? For many, a need to pay the rent and eat, clearly. But that's not all. Few of us who live in the Western world *must* do exactly what we do to feed and clothe ourselves. Many times our career choices are really more influenced by a cocktail of duty, fear, apathy, talent, priorities, and passion. Alternate lives, at least one or two of them, often lie within reach.

"What keeps me here?" I repeated. "I feel as if I wandered onto this path and I'm never quite sure it's the right one for me to be on. But I think it almost helps to know that I have other options I *could* pursue if I chose to. That steadies me. It helps me say: 'For better or for worse. For adventure or for email. For now. I chose this.'"

"How long do you think you'll keep choosing this?" Erica asked.

"I don't know," I said. "I still can't see myself here long term – L.A. is not my home. But I love my job, I've got good friends here, and perhaps for the first time in my life, I've decided that I need a better reason to leave than an intangible restlessness and the sense that I don't quite belong."

This resolve to fight the restlessness and ignore the temptation of other paths was a huge paradigm shift for me. It was also a decision that would shortly be tested. Barely two months after this conversation with Erica, a stranger's email would startle me into wondering whether that better reason to leave might have just landed in my inbox.

Los Angeles – Accra – Washington, D.C. – Sydney – Zagreb – South Bend – Nairobi – San Diego – **Atlanta** – **Madang** – Kona – Canberra – London – Baltimore – Itonga – Vancouver – Harare – Dushanbe – Lira – Petats – Port Moresby – Brisbane – Ballina – Malibu

IN THE BEGINNING WERE THE WORDS

Los Angeles, USA

I WAS AT ERICA'S house when the letter arrived.

We were all still in our pajamas at 9 a.m. I was at the kitchen table on my laptop. Leah was lying flat on the floor in the long ray of sunshine falling through the bay window. Erica was rinsing coffee mugs and trying to talk us into finding the energy to go to the L.A. farmers market.

"Huh," I said when I opened the email.

"What?" Erica asked when I didn't say anything else.

"This guy," I eventually answered, still scanning down the page. "There's this guy in Papua New Guinea, and he's just sent me a really long letter."

Leah lifted her head off the floor and raised an eyebrow.

Erica wasn't amused either.

"New Guinea? Where do you find these people?" she asked.

"Hey!" I said, deciding the letter would keep for a while and shutting down my computer. It was not the most sophisticated of comebacks, but I wasn't in any position from the little I'd read to argue that this letter already felt different from some of the other missives I'd received since the novel I'd finally finished had been published two months earlier.

"Have you heard from that other guy again?" Leah asked.

"Lust-thrust guy?" I asked.

Lust-thrust guy was becoming a regular conversation topic among friends. I was starting to regret having told anyone about him, but when the first email arrived, I'd just been puzzled and amused by the opening gambit. "I came across a pamphlet near my mailbox," this stranger wrote, "and while browsing through the book summaries your photo caught my eye. It was love-phase-1 at first glance."

Seriously?

No, seriously??

That was my reaction until the second letter arrived two weeks later, after my first reading at a local bookstore.

The knowledge that he'd been in the audience gave me my first shiver. The poem he finished his letter with gave me my second, and it didn't take more than the first two lines:

"Dust to dust, I wander in the lust,
You gave the dreams, how about the thrust?"

I'd laughed about this with my friends.

But then the next letter, titled *Divine Chemistry,* arrived two weeks later.

Then another letter, two weeks after that.

And I stopped finding it funny.

I never answered any of these letters, and lust-thrust guy eventually stopped writing to me. I, however, never quite stopped scanning for his face in the audience whenever I did a local reading.

The letter I'd just received on that sunny fall morning was different, though, I was sure. For one thing, I hadn't seen any creepy rhymes in my quick perusal. For another, I recognized his name – Mike had written to me before. The previous Tuesday a note from someone named Mike who lived in Papua New Guinea had dropped out of nowhere into my work email account, right in the middle of a very busy day.

Atlanta, USA

THE SEED OF MIKE'S first letter to me was planted not in Papua New Guinea but in Atlanta.

In Atlanta, a stranger named Erin, an acquiring editor for a magazine, had received a press release about my novel. As she scanned the synopsis and my author biography, it wasn't my book that had held her attention – it was my day job as a stress-management trainer for humanitarian workers. Erin thought of her old friend Mike, who was a humanitarian worker in Papua New Guinea, and figured she should sign him up for the Headington Institute newsletter.

So Erin went to my writing website and looked for a link to the Headington Institute. What she discovered first, however, were my essays. Several essays later, Erin found that she wasn't as interested in hooking Mike up with the institute newsletter as she was in hooking him up with me.

Yes, Erin acknowledged as she thought it through, the fact that I lived in Los Angeles could prove to be a minor drawback. But she also knew by now that I had grown up a country-hopping nomad. My upbringing, she reasoned, had prepared me well for the challenging romantic equation she was visualizing.

As for Mike, as she told him months later, "I was so overcome with giddiness at striking gold via one glossy sheet of press mess that I had to brag to the people in the nearest three cubicles that I had just found the perfect woman for my friend in Papua New Guinea."

So Erin wrote to Mike that day and strongly encouraged him to look at my website.

Mike rolled his eyes and wrote back to Erin. He lived in a small town in Papua New Guinea with unreliable dial-up internet, he pointed out. He wasn't about to go browsing the website of a stranger living in L.A., a stranger Erin wasn't even sure was single.

Undeterred, Erin downloaded all the essays on my website, compiled them into a sixty-page document and emailed it to Mike.

Mike groaned but, other entertainment options being in short supply, started reading.

After he was finished, dial-up connection notwithstanding, Mike visited my website. As the photo on my homepage slowly scrolled open, Mike realized that he'd seen my face the week before, on the Facebook page of a friend he'd met six years earlier in Melbourne.

Mike decided to drop me a line.

Los Angeles, USA

MIKE'S FIRST LETTER – a casual note mentioning our mutual friend, Alison, and asking to be added to my email list – hit my inbox in the middle of a less-than-placid day at work.

I didn't have much time to pause and wonder how my essays

had found their way to a remote corner of Papua New Guinea, but I did snatch a couple of minutes two days later to send a brief reply and, on a whim, a friend request on Facebook. Mike's thumbnail picture on the site was so small I couldn't really make out what he looked like, but when I'd searched his name, Facebook had proudly informed me that Alison wasn't our only mutual friend.

Mike was also friends with Alison's husband, Paul, and several of Paul's siblings. I'd gotten to know Paul's family as a teenager when both of our families had lived in Zimbabwe. Paul was my first real crush. At fifteen, I was convinced I wanted to marry the brooding, mysterious seventeen-year-old.

But Paul wasn't even the weirdest thread in our tangle of indirect connections.

Mike was also linked to another friend of mine, Ryan. Ryan was living in Afghanistan and churning out raw and compelling essays of his own when, completely infatuated with his writing, I first tracked him down via email and pestered him until he gave in and agreed to be my friend.

But back to Mike.

Five days after Mike sent his first note.

Three days after I answered it.

The letter – a letter that showed me that he'd read my essays very carefully indeed – arrived.

Madang, Papua New Guinea

Sunday, October 21
From: Mike Wolfe
To: Lisa McKay
Subject: A breath of fresh air

Hi Lisa,

It's a partly cloudy afternoon. As I sit at my dining room table, Ella Fitzgerald on iTunes is competing with the upbeat Pacific rhythms coming from across the street. Our neighbor across the fence is having some sort of public meeting in his backyard, so every now and then fifteen men clap their hands enthusiastically. We used to think the regular Saturday meetings were political in nature, but the elections have come and gone and the men continue to gather. I'm a bit curious. But getting the answer would require me not only to walk all the way across the lawn, but also make the effort to introduce myself properly to the man of the house instead of my normal practice of smiling and nodding at him in the mornings when I jog by. Right now I just can't be bothered to make that additional effort.

So a dear friend in Atlanta, Erin, compiled all your online essays into one compact document so that I didn't have to labor with my dial-up connection to read them.

I really enjoyed journeying with you through your essays. I contemplated. I laughed. I commiserated. I felt moved. I felt challenged. I felt comforted and consoled in the way that one feels consoled when one reads that he is not the only being on the planet who experiences being thirty-one and talented, and purpose-driven, and questioning whether the road less traveled is worth the opportunity cost of the greener grass on the other side of the fence. And whether it's really worth it, searching for goodness and hope in the midst of some shitty shit in this world. And feeling crap about it all some of the time and feeling really joyful sometimes, too. And being tossed around by vacillating feelings, and perplexing questions, and unrealized hopes, and longing for things to be right (whatever that means). Also, longing for a nice big bowl of ice cream. And a bottle of Barossa

Shiraz shared with good friends.

Reading your essays was a breath of fresh air to my spirit. Thanks.

It's kinda funny that after journeying with you in your essays, I feel like I know you. Which, of course, my non-psychology training tells me is most likely me projecting my needs and wants onto another person. Which is just oh sooooo helpful in life's various flavors of relationships.

Because allow me to be straightforward here and say that I'd like to know more about Lisa McKay. I feel like I know some of your personality, but ?? You have gorgeous eyes and a great smile. I even quite like your blue passport, although I don't need it. I already have my own blue American passport that allows me to traipse all over the world. But I do love Australia.

Of course, I have some trepidation as I write – "apprehension" or "misgivings" would work as well – about whether it's even worth it to expose oneself to the potential ordeals that a relationship between LA and PNG would entail. My one data point of experience in this long-distance relationship matter culminated in making a phone call to Indonesia from Sri Lanka and having the woman I thought I may just marry break up with me because she realized (correctly it turns out) that it just wasn't going to work for us. Hence apprehensions and misgivings.

Now this is all the more crazy because Tuesday I'm heading out to spend the next two months in Vanuatu and Solomon Islands, and most of my time will be spent in remote villages without email and electricity (and perhaps even without Coca-Cola, but I doubt it).

But hey, why shy away from challenges?

So give it a think and decide what you'd like to do. And drop me a line when you like. No worries. Really. Regardless of what you say, I'm not going to turn into a Lisa stalker.

Acknowledging the imbalance of information between us, I feel that I ought to ("ought" in the non-guilt sense) share some Mike info. I used to be quite a regular mass e-mailer once upon a traumatic first humanitarian posting in Central Asia. Alas, my writing skills have atrophied over the years. I have but one mass email from PNG that I've attached. And they say that a picture is worth a thousand words. I don't buy it, but I've also attached a link to the thirty photos from thirty countries that I displayed at my 30th birthday party last year.

Well, Ella has long stopped playing, the meeting across the fence has ended and I've rambled for quite a few paragraphs as I am prone to do. But I meant every word.

Drop me a line when you like. No rush. And keep on writing. You're quite good at it.

Cheers from PNG,
Mike

Los Angeles, USA

I DIDN'T READ THIS letter carefully until after I'd driven home from Erica's on Sunday afternoon. I will share most things with Erica and Leah without hesitating, so I don't know exactly what it was that made me flip my laptop closed on that sunny fall morning in Erica's kitchen and save Mike's letter for later.

Why, right from the start, did this letter seem different?

It wasn't just that Mike said he liked my essays. Other people had said they liked my essays, although few could relate the way he clearly could.

Perhaps that was it, or part of it. The photographs he'd sent made it clear that Mike had traveled the world during the last decade. I suspected that anyone who could survive postings in Tajikistan, Uganda, Sri Lanka, and PNG in short order was either seriously crazy or seriously interesting. And given that the letter he'd attached about bush life in PNG was relaxed, confident, and seasoned with *joie de vivre*, I would have put money on seriously interesting.

He was cute, too. He was in only one of the thirty photos he'd put together for his birthday celebration, but it was a beauty. He was kneeling, surrounded by children in Rwanda, looking at them instead of the camera. His eyes were green, his smile wide.

Who has the power to stay untouched by *that?*

I certainly didn't, but I was nervous, too. I hadn't dated anyone in three years, not since my last long-distance relationship had derailed in painful slow motion.

Dating? Wait just one minute! Am I out of my mind??

Mike and I had exchanged a grand total of three emails, I reminded myself. There was an 18-hour time difference and about seven thousand miles between us. We had jobs we loved anchoring us on different sides of the world, he had spotty internet access, and we'd be starting from the ground up with these constraints already in place. If I'd ever heard of an against-the-odds long-distance scenario, this was it. Why was I even *thinking* the word *dating?*

I knew it didn't make the slightest bit of sense, but I was. There was no getting around it. The next night I settled down to see if I could corral these thoughts into a coherent reply.

Monday, October 22
From: Lisa McKay
To: Mike Wolfe
Subject: Re: A breath of fresh air

Hi Mike,

It's a mellow evening. I'm on the couch. The pumpkin's oiled, salted, and in the oven. The door's open to let the tail end of the eighty-degree day into the house, and I remembered that there was a whole case of red wine buried in the storage closet in the garage after I thought we were out and the pasta sauce was going to have to be wine-less. Happy days.

It seems, however, that I have not drunk enough of that wine yet to stem the sudden shyness I am feeling. Yes, I know, it seems silly. I write these essays and put them online. I am choosing to live out part of my life in an incredibly public forum. But to find out that people are reading them and resonating on some primal level ... well. That is profoundly exciting and validating and comforting in that inner essential loneliness, but it's also scary. Because I know it's an edited version of me that goes into those essays. All the boring parts, all those days and moments when I'm flat or exhausted or grumpy or uninspiring or selfish ... they get cut out. I know I'm not as interesting or witty as those essays make me appear when read in a vacuum (not to mention not as attractive as the press photos for the book might imply).

So your letter yesterday morning both startled me and made me smile. I'm flattered and intrigued but, like you it seems, wary. My points of reference with regard to long-distance relationships have not ended in happily ever after either. One attempt that started with a premature and reckless intensity ended in a tangled mess, with his heart broken and me discovering I had serious conflict-avoidance tendencies in romantic relationships. A second attempt taught me the very important lesson that the living, breathing someone will inevitably turn out to be very different from the idealized someone who springs to life in my head when I read their writing.

So, all that said, I don't know much about you except that you have good taste in friends, have chosen to live and work in a field that has captured my passions, are game to ride in trucks on dirt roads and sleep in huts, are probably largely fueled by those twin forces of adventure and purpose-seeking, have an eye for photography, and have a smile that suggests warm and friendly.

I would like to get to know you better. So if you're game, let's email. As friends. Or as people who think they might want to become friends. With no expectations of anything more until we at least cross paths in person, if we ever get there.

And as for inaccessibility over the next two months, I leave on Sunday for a month on the road myself. I'm off to Kenya, then Ghana, then back to Baltimore. My life is officially scheduled to be insane until the 28th of November. Then I have about a month in L.A. before I'm off to Australia for a holiday. So, yeah, I get the whole out-of-touch thing. But when you are near electricity and the www and fueled up on Coca-Cola, I look forward to hearing how your trip is going and what started you on this path in the first place. How did you end up in PNG from Pennsylvania? Where's home?

And now I must get off the couch, check on that pumpkin, and put the rest of the red wine to good use in the pasta sauce.

Cheers,
Lisa

During the next week, before Mike and I got on planes and headed for parts beyond the reach of the worldwide web, we exchanged thirteen thousand words. And in those rapid-fire exchanges I learned a great deal about Mike.

He'd grown up on a small family farm in Pennsylvania, almost as isolated from pop culture then as he was now. The farm and his parents were responsible for instilling in him a German-Puritanesque work ethic that still haunted him. Although, he said, he felt he'd made great strides in his work-life balance strategies in recent times. He used to arrive at work between 5:30 and 6 a.m., and now he aimed for 7, you see.

Bent on embracing solidarity with the poor, Mike had followed a passion for justice into aid work by taking a volunteer posting in Tajikistan, and he promised that story later – a story of "light, darkness, hope, angst and wonder all intertwined." His current posting in Papua New Guinea was raising the quintessential humanitarian-worker dilemma:

> "My heart screams, 'I hate this complicated messy type of work and I'm sick and tired of being so damn lonely and why can't I just go get a job somewhere normal (whatever that is)?' but my brain says, 'It's good, stick with it, it's worthwhile.' The shorter version is that my emotions vacillate wildly. My emotions are real. But the way I feel at any given moment isn't the exhaustive truth about the world. And so, God, please give me wisdom, grace, endurance, patience, hope, and joy. Please, God."

He liked red wine and dark chocolate.

Planes still filled him with the excited sense that he was headed for adventure.

His letters made me laugh.

I learned some things about myself that week, too. I already knew that I was a sucker for funny, chatty, emails written by people irresistibly attracted to challenge. But I learned that Mike's frank expression of interest and the boundary lines I'd drawn in the sand freed me to be relaxed and openly, casually honest in ways I'd never been with a man before. And I learned that I wasn't sure I had a good answer for one of the first questions I was asking Mike.

Where is home?

I was still thinking this issue through when I got on the plane to Kenya.

Los Angeles – **Accra** – Washington, D.C. – Sydney – Zagreb – South
Bend – **Nairobi** – San Diego – Atlanta – Madang – **Kona** – **Canberra** –
London – Baltimore – Itonga – Vancouver – Harare – Dushanbe – Lira
– Petats – Port Moresby – Brisbane – Ballina – Malibu

AIRPORTS AND BOOKSTORES

*"Home is a name, a word, it is a strong one; stronger than
magician ever spoke, or spirit ever answered to, in the strongest
conjuration."*

(Charles Dickens)

Nairobi, Kenya

I LANDED IN KENYA twenty-eight hours after I left California.

It was 9 p.m.

It was dark.

It's less than completely desirable to land in Nairobi in the
dark. There's only one road linking the airport with the city.
It's not unheard of for vehicles to be ambushed on that road,
especially at night, and not everyone offering to be a taxi driver
at that airport can be counted on to have the purest of intentions
regarding your valuables or your person.

After years of traveling the world solo, I might be rather too casual about the specifics of my itinerary sometimes, but I do know enough never to treat travel by car in Nairobi lightly. I'd arranged with my hotel to have a trusted driver at the airport to greet me, and the hotel manager had given me specific instructions regarding the driver's identification. He'd be carrying a sign with the hotel logo, the manager wrote, and wearing a green badge with his name stamped on it in white.

I saw the sign easily enough as I exited customs, and a wide smile, but no badge.

"Ah!" he said. "You are the Lisa!"

Where, I inquired with a smile of my own as we shook hands, was his badge?

In the car, Willy the driver confessed conspiratorially. The others would tease him, you see, if he wore it. There would be no end to the laughing and the calling out of his name by the hundreds of other men thronging the arrivals area.

"Hey, Willy!" he demonstrated for me. "Hey, my brother, Willy! Yes my friend, will you be taking me in your taxi, *Willy*?"

I sighed. If the word *willy* meant the same thing in Kenya that it did in Australia, I was sure that was not all that the mocking throngs did with his name.

"Okay," I said as I followed him out into the night. "But I can see the badge at the car, yes?"

Yes.

There was no trouble on the drive into the city from the airport; the only unexpected sight was a herd of zebras. They flashed past, stripy and gorgeous in the headlights. It was so dry here right now, Willy explained, that they were jumping the game-park fences and wandering into the city outskirts, desperate for water.

"Are things quiet here?" I asked as we left the thirsty zebras behind and continued on into the darkness.

Willy knew what I was asking about, the post-election violence that had surprised Kenya and the rest of the world nine months before and left more than a thousand dead.

"Oh, yes," he reassured me. "Very calm."

The area where Willy lived had been hit hard by the rioting, but he hadn't lost his house or any of his family. He had, however, seemed to have lost any faith he once possessed in his government, or democracy, or perhaps both.

He would never vote again, he said.

"What is the point?" Willy said. "You get up before the day comes and line up all day in the sun to vote, and in the end it means nothing and you can lose everything – your home, your family, your life. Everything, eh? Everything."

There were many things I wanted to ask him in the car that night, not least of which was why he believed that not voting was the best way to prevent such violence from happening again. But I felt too tired and too foreign to formulate that question with appropriate tact, and in the end Willy didn't give me the space to try.

"Where is your home?" he asked me.

Five years ago whenever someone asked me this question I'd launch into a long list, rushing to pack it all in before their eyes glazed over. I was born in Canada but my parents were Australian, I'd explain. Then we moved to Australia. Then Bangladesh. Then Washington, D.C. Then Zimbabwe, the U.S., and Australia again. Oh, and Indonesia.

Three years ago when someone asked me this question, more often than not I'd simply freeze.

Lately I've been embracing simplicity. And brevity. I seem to finally be losing the need to assault strangers with my own uncertainty around this issue.

"California," I told Willy. "I live in Los Angeles."

"Oh!" Willy said, impressed. "Lots of movie stars, eh?"

Yes.

"This is your first time to Kenya?"

No, I told him. This was my fifth trip here in five years. I was here to run workshops on stress and trauma for aid workers.

"You see and hear a lot of terrible things when you work for humanitarian organizations," I said.

Willy fell silent. I wondered whether he was thinking that someone should come run those workshops for Nairobi's taxi drivers.

"You could hear it, the shooting and the yelling," Willy said, and I knew his mind had jumped back in time, to the terrible uncertainty of January and February. "You could hear it from my home. My neighbors, eh … How can you forgive the people, afterward, those ones that killed your family, your parents? How can you forgive those ones? No, that forgiving—that is not possible. It is better just to forget those terrible things. Everyone, they want to forget. They do not want to talk about it. Except, maybe it is that you *look* like you forget, but you do not. And in ten years, or twenty years maybe, those things they come back. And then there is the revenge. You like Kenya?" he demanded, suddenly switching tack.

"Yes," I said honestly, "I like coming to Kenya. I've been here so often that now it feels a little like coming home."

But even as I used that troublesome last word, *home*, I felt an internal tickle. A sense that I might be blaspheming something that I do not yet fully understand.

Willy, however, liked it.

"Ah," he said. "That is good. This is a very good. *Karibu*. You are welcome."

"*Asante sana*," I said, using about half the Swahili that I know in that one exchange.

Thank you.

Kona, USA

THE FACT THAT I might have a real problem when it came to this concept of home didn't occur to me until I was twenty-six years old.

I was having the time of my life at the first creative writing workshop I'd ever attended. A friend had linked me up with accommodation for ten bucks a night, I was surrounded by people who *loved* to write and, as a bonus, I was in Hawaii.

During the first week I didn't have much trouble with any of the writing assignments we were given in class. We had to write about two people meeting on a beach when one of them was self-conscious about being seen in a bathing suit, or create a scene where what one of the characters said and what he actually meant were very different. These sorts of exercises came relatively easily. It wasn't until day seven that I really stumbled.

Borrowing inspiration from the tale of the prodigal son in the Bible, our instructors had told us to write a "coming home" story. We should, we were told, write the prodigal who was us as an adult, coming home to ourselves as a child.

"Pick the clearest recollection you have of home and use that," they said.

Everyone else reached for a pen or a laptop. I just sat there.

I was still sitting there ten minutes later.

Eventually I went up to the front of the room, to the giant leather-bound book of synonyms that was sitting on a podium, looked up *home* and wrote down these words: *Birthplace. Stability. Dwelling. Hearth. Hearthstone. Refuge. Shelter. Haven. Sanctum.*

I went back to my seat and stared past the book of synonyms, past the palm trees standing still under a blanket of midday heat, and out into the hazy blue of an ocean that promised a horizon it never quite delivered.

The list didn't seem to help much.

Birthplace conjured Vancouver, a city I'd visited only twice, briefly, since we'd left when I was one.

Stability then. Unlike my parents', not a word that could be applied to my childhood. In stark contrast with their agrarian upbringing, I'd spent an awful lot of my time in airports.

Maybe that was it, I thought, wondering whether the sudden spark I felt at the word *airport* was a glimmer of inspiration or merely desperation.

There was no denying that as a child I'd thought there was a lot of fun to be had in and around airports. More than one home movie shows me and Michelle arranging our stuffed animals and secondhand Barbies in symmetrical rows and lecturing them severely about seat belts and tray tables before offering to serve them drinks. When we were actually *in* airports, we spent many happy hours collecting luggage carts and returning them to the distribution stands in order to pocket the deposit. We were always very disappointed to find ourselves in those boring socialist airports with free trolleys.

Money was a bit of a recurring theme in my childhood airport adventures. Traveling out of Bangladesh one time, Michelle and I procured an in-flight blanket and draped it over our two-year-old brother. We then persuaded the agreeable blond cherub to toddle off and beg from the other passengers in Bengali. "Baksheesh? Baksheesh?" Matthew said, his green eyes and dimples irresistible. As I recall, we got some money out of the exercise, which my scandalized and exhausted parents made us return when they figured out what we were up to.

In Hawaii, I was tempted to start writing my story about home but didn't.

"Your clearest memories of home as a child cannot possibly be in an airport," I scolded myself, still staring past my laptop and out to the white-laced toss and chop of cerulean. "Home is not a topic that deserves flippancy. Work harder. ... What about dwellings and hearths?"

That year my parents were living in the Philippines. Matthew was in Sydney. Michelle was in Washington, D.C. The bed I could legitimately call mine resided in Indiana. I had lived none of these places except D.C. as a child, and *they* were such awkward, lonely years that the thought of going back, even in a story, made me squirm. We lived in Washington, D.C., for three and a half years before moving to Zimbabwe, and what I remember most clearly about that time is that I spent much of it reading.

I've been in love with reading since before I can remember. Our family photo albums are peppered with photos of me curled up with books – in huts in Bangladesh, on trains in Europe, in the backseat of our car in Zimbabwe.

I can't remember my parents reading to us before bed, although they swear they often did – sweet tales about poky puppies and confused baby birds looking for their mothers.

"You were insatiable," Mum said when I asked her about this once. "No matter how many times I read you a book, you always wanted more."

"Awwww," I said, envisioning long rainy afternoons curled up with my mother while she read to me. "You must have spent *hours* reading to me."

"I *did*," my mother said in a tone that let me know she fully expects me to return the favor one day. "But it was never enough. So I taped myself."

"What?" I asked.

"I got a tape recorder," she said. "I recorded myself reading a story – I even put these cute little chimes in there so you'd know when to turn the page. Then, sometimes, I sat you down with the tapes."

"Nice," I said in a way that let her know that I didn't think this practice would get her nominated for the motherly hall of fame.

"You loved it," she said, completely uncowed. "Plus, I needed a break every now and then. You were exhausting. You never stopped asking questions. You asked thirty-seven questions once during a half-hour episode of Lassie. I counted."

I can't remember any of this. My earliest memories of reading are solitary, sweaty ones. They are of lying on the cool marble floor of our house in Bangladesh, book in hand, an overhead fan gently stirring the dense heat while I chipped away at frozen applesauce in a small plastic container. But it's when we moved from Bangladesh to the states when I was nine that my memories of books, just like childhood itself, become clearer.

Of all the moves I've made in my life, this was one of the most traumatic. Abruptly encountering the world of the very wealthy after two years of living cheek by jowl with the world of the very poor, I discovered that I didn't fit readily into either world. My fourth grade classmates in Washington D.C. had no framework for understanding where I had been for the last two years – what it was like to ride to church in a rickshaw pulled by a skinny man on a bicycle, to make a game out of pulling three-inch-long cockroaches out of the sink drain while brushing your teeth at night, or to gaze from the windows of your school bus at other children picking through the corner garbage dumps.

I, in turn, lacked the inclination to rapidly absorb and adopt the rules of this new world, a world where your grasp on preteen fashion, pop culture, and boys all mattered terribly. Possibly I could have compensated for my almost total lack of knowledge in these key areas with lashings of gregarious charm, but at nine I lacked that, too. I was not what you would call a sunny child.

So I read instead. I read desperately.

I read pretty much anything I could get my hands on. One of the few good things I could see about living in the states was the ready availability of books. Some weekends Mum and Dad would take us to the local library's used-book sale. Books were a quarter each. I had a cardboard box and carte blanche. On those Saturday mornings I was in heaven.

Like many kids, I suspect, I was drawn to stories of outsiders or children persevering against all odds in the face of hardship. I devoured all of C.S. Lewis' stories of Narnia and adored the novels of Frances Hodgson Burnett, especially the ones featuring little girls who were raised in India before being exiled to face great hardship in Britain. But I also strayed into more adult territory. I trolled our bookshelves and the bookshelves of family friends, and those bookshelves were gold mines for stories about everything from religious persecution to murder, rape, civil war, child brides, and honor killing.

"It would be nice," my father commented dryly upon reading the first draft of this chapter, "if you could manage *not* to make it sound like our personal library was stocked exclusively with troubling filth."

"Dad," I explained, "that's why I used the gold-mine analogy. You don't just stumble across gold; you have to dig for it. I worked really hard to find that stuff in amongst all the boring family-friendly fare you were prone to buying."

Mum and Dad didn't know everything I got into, of course. After they caught me reading a tale set largely in a brothel in South Africa and confiscated it, I got stealthier with censorable material. I also found their hiding place – behind the pile of sweaters on the top shelf of the wardrobe – and read the rest of that particular book in chunks during times when they were both out of the house.

In retrospect, even at eleven I wasn't reading largely for pleasant diversion, for fun, for the literary equivalent of eating ice cream in the middle of the day. I was extreme-reading – pushing boundaries – looking to be shocked, scared, thrilled, and taught. I was reading to try to figure out how to make sense of pain.

It is entirely possible that had we remained in Australia throughout my childhood, I would still have spent the majority of these preteen years feeling isolated and misunderstood. After all, in the midst of our mobility I never doubted my parents' love for me or for each other, but this did not forestall an essential loneliness that was very deeply felt. I suspect that I would still have grown into someone who feels compelled to explore the juxtaposition of shadow and light, someone who is drawn to discover what lies in the dark of life and of ourselves. But I also suspect that the shocking extremes presented by life in Bangladesh and America propelled me down this path earlier, and farther, than I may naturally have ventured.

It was largely books that were my early companions on this journey. They were stories of poverty and struggle, injustice and abuse, violence and debauchery, yes. But they were also threaded through with honor and courage, sacrifice and discipline, character and hope.

Many people seem to view "real life" as the gold standard by which to interpret stories, but I don't think that does novels justice. For me, at least, the relationship between the real and fictional worlds was reciprocal. These books named emotions, pointed to virtue and vice, and led me into a deeper understanding of things I had already witnessed and experienced myself. They also let me try on, like a child playing dress-up, experiences and notions new to me. They acted as maps, mirrors, and magnifying glasses.

In those lonely childhood years, books also provided refuge. They were havens and sanctums.

Did that make them home?

When the writing exercise ended after half an hour and we were invited to share, I'd come up with only two ideas.

Set the scene in a bookstore. Or set it in an airport.

I hadn't written a single word.

Canberra, Australia

PERHAPS ONE OF THE reasons I got so stuck in Hawaii when asked to write about home is that my images of what home *should* be are so firmly anchored in place. But how can you have a firm sense of a place as home when you've moved a dozen times and your longest stint in any single city was from age one to seven? I can barely even remember that house in Canberra.

There was a giant dog that lived next door, some sort of Great Dane mix. It was as big as a small horse, and I was both fascinated and terrified by its majestic, seemingly placid presence.

A bird flew into the kitchen window one day with a tremendous bang and broke its neck. We buried the limp still-warm body in the garden in a shoe box and marked the grave with a cross made out of popsicle sticks.

I shared a bedroom with my little sister. There was a foam couch between our beds that we used as a bridge for silent post-bedtime acrobatics. Michelle fell one night and took a chunk out of her eyebrow on the metal frame of her bed. Blood fountained.

Mum and Dad were not impressed. That was the end of our late-night acrobatics.

I find it a little disturbing that the only clear memories I have of my first real home in Canberra were apparently imprinted there by fear, death, or injury. The details of happiness, it seems, take longer to settle in.

Los Angeles, USA

I ASKED MY SISTER and brother about this shortly after I moved to Los Angeles. Through part happy accident and part good trans-continental schedule coordination, they both managed to visit L.A. on the same weekend. New to L.A. myself at that stage, I cast around for something cool for the three of us to do and settled on the Huntington Gardens.

That Saturday we took a picnic blanket and wandered around those green and manicured acres – through the rose garden, past the prickly and bulbous cacti, and down a long shady pathway that wound through a stand of bamboo. At the very bottom of the park, past a pond jammed with lilies, we found what we were looking for: the Australian section.

We spread our picnic blanket on the grass under the gum trees and lay down. Pale bark hung off the trunks in papery sheets, and, above, dry gunmetal leaves rustled in the breeze. I took a deep breath, searching for the eucalyptus signature, menthol.

I can't remember which of the three of us suggested calling Mum and Dad, but it was probably Michelle. Michelle tends to be the one who remembers things like the fact that it would warm the cockles of our parents' peripatetic little hearts to know that we were all together in the Australian section of the Hungtington Gardens.

"We can't call the parentals," Matt said. "We only have a mobile phone."

"We can," Michelle and I said at the same time and then looked at each other and laughed.

"I've got Mum and Dad's calling-card number memorized," I said proudly, since memorizing any string of digits is a noteworthy achievement for me.

"Me, too," Michelle said.

Matt did not give us the applause I thought was warranted.

"Are you two *still* using Mum and Dad's calling card?" he asked.

"What?" I said. "Mum and Dad don't care, as long as we also use it to call them."

Matt looked at me in silence, with eyes narrowed and just the merest contemplative curl to his lips. Matt is very good at communicating in silence. This particular silence said something like "Don't you think, my dear sister, that perhaps it's time you got your own international calling card?"

I answered him out loud.

"Aren't Mum and Dad still paying for your car registration and insurance?"

Matt's wide grin appeared with all the sweet suddenness of the sun coming out from behind clouds.

"That's my tax for staying in Australia," he said. "With you two both gone, they're pretty happy to have *one* of us still there."

"Does Australia feel like home yet?" I asked. Like both Michelle and me before him, after spending childhood and adolescence abroad, Matt had returned to Australia to attend university. He'd now been back for about four years.

"I don't know," Matt said slowly, shrugging. "I mean, we left when I was one. What's home supposed to feel like?"

I recognized the inarticulate confusion I'd stirred up and

rerouted, jumping to something else I'd been thinking through recently.

"Do you guys remember much about early childhood?" I asked. "I feel like I can't remember as much about it as other people say they can. Some people talk about remembering things from when they were two or three, but I struggle to remember anything much clearly before five, at the earliest."

"Me, too," Matt said. "My memory's crap."

"Mine, too!" Michelle said. "I can hardly remember anything from Bangladesh, and I was seven when we left! I was just talking about this in counseling the other day."

Michelle paused then, looking pensive.

Of the three of us, Michelle had made the most definitive decisions about the place she would call home. The previous year, she had married her high school sweetheart, Jed, and moved back to Maryland. This transition hadn't been entirely smooth, and as she'd essentially adopted America, Michelle decided that she might as well experiment with one of the common cultural mores and try seeing a counselor as well. From the little I'd heard, I was dubious as to whether this woman was going to be a good fit.

"What'd she say?" I asked.

"She ..." Michelle paused again. "She said childhood memory loss is common in abuse cases."

"She said *what*?!?" I asked, sitting up.

"She also wants you to come to a session with me next time you're in town," Michelle continued. "She thinks it might help her understand me better."

"I *cannot* believe that she *suggested to you* that you may have been abused as a child in your second session with her," I said. "That is so dodgy."

"I'd never even thought about it before, but do you think

it's even a possibility?" Michelle asked, trying – and almost succeeding – to sound as if my answer wasn't that important.

"It's *possible*, I guess," I said. "But it's unlikely. Total amnesia about abuse does happen, but it's really not all that common. Plus, all three of us have the same problem and we certainly weren't being abused at home. Did she consider that perhaps a lot of moving around as a child disrupted your ability to lay down early memories?"

"No," Michelle said. "Just abuse. So will you come to counseling with me next time you're in town?"

"Yes," I said, lying back down and looking up through the leaves. As was often the case in L.A., there wasn't a cloud in sight.

"In the meantime," I said, "just tell her that when we were little and people asked you questions, I used to tell them that you didn't talk, then I'd answer for you. And I don't think that you said the word *no* to me until you were twelve. Also, I used to hide in your closet occasionally while you were brushing your teeth at night and wait until you were in bed and it was all dark and then jump out and scare you. I am very sorry about all of this now, truly I am. But I do not believe it constitutes child abuse of the type your counselor is probably thinking about."

"You got off lightly," Matt reminded Michelle. "She told me I was adopted."

"Awww," I said, smiling at the memory. "I did. I even made you a fake birth certificate."

"Okay," Michelle said, clearly happy to let this go for the time being. "Shall we call Mum and Dad?"

"Yes. Let's ask them whether *they* think you were abused as a child," I said.

"That is not funny," Matt said sternly. "And do you want to give Dad nightmares for a week? Even without the prospect of abuse, I reckon he'd still be upset to think that we couldn't remember things as well because of all the moving around."

"Why?" I said. "Are we not allowed to acknowledge that growing up leapfrogging borders may just have come with some price tags attached? Does it *all* have to be positive? Would any of us trade our experiences despite those price tags?"

———— ∞∞ ————

MY MEMORY IMPROVED WITH time. I do better with recalling our later houses.

Brown carpet here, marble floors there. Here a kidney-shaped swimming pool, there a swing set or a courtyard. Windows sternly barred with black metal, or white wood clutching small clear panes, or great glossy sheets of shatterproof glass that looked out from the 27th floor and didn't even open.

These places were all homes in their own fashion. They just weren't *home,* singular.

That was probably my other problem in Hawaii. I've always had this sense that home *should* be singular. That you really have only one.

When I put these two ideas together – the singularity of place that I've burdened the concept of home with – I understand better why from this vantage point nowhere I've ever lived looks fully like home to me. It has less to do with whether that place *felt* like a home during the time I lived there than with there being about a dozen such places.

Accra, Ghana

TEN DAYS INTO MY latest Africa trip, I found myself eating alone at the hotel in Ghana.

It was a precious pause during what was turning out to be a

draining stint.

Overall, the workshops in Kenya had gone well. There were the usual challenges, of course. Jet lag and nightmares prodded me awake at 3 a.m. on my second night in country and left me lying there thrumming with fatigue and questioning my decision to embark on this line of work in the first place, whether anything I do really makes a difference, and whether I'm actually worth *anything* as a human being.

Those are really fun hours, those ones.

Then there were the late nights filled with the tedium of organizing handouts and name tags. During the workshops, there was a plethora of unexpected questions from the group, including, bizarrely, in the middle of a discussion of stress and spirituality, "Can you explain the stress of menopause?"

Every international assignment, however, teaches me again what makes the long flights, the 3 a.m. angst, and the huge amount of energy it takes to facilitate worth it. These are amazing people who sit in these workshops. They are people who have chosen to work in the slums and help children to stay in school instead of unwittingly embracing life sentences of boredom, menial labor, or crime by dropping out. They are lawyers who prosecute case after case of child sexual abuse or land-grabbing. They are people who have made careers of documenting the stories of refugees in camps all over Africa who are desperate for a chance at another life. Persecution histories, these stories are called, and they are largely tales of horror and fear.

This was the group I was working with in Ghana, people who spend much of their time in camps in West Africa interviewing an endless stream of displaced people seeking refugee status and resettlement in the United States. The first day's workshop on understanding and coping with traumatic

stress had been lively. This group was also full of interesting
questions like "What should I do when a refugee I'm
interviewing starts showing me their wounds or demands that
I touch them?" And "When someone is obliquely referring to
having been raped, should I use the word *rape* or mirror their
language? How can I encourage them to give more details
without breaching cultural taboos around rape and causing
further shame?"

When faced with questions like these, I sometimes use a
facilitation technique I could call "tapping into the collective
wisdom of the group."

Of course, I could also call it "In this exact moment I have
no idea how to address that well, so let's ask everyone else
present what they think."

There is little spare time on one of these international work
trips. From the time I hit the ground, I'm usually absorbed in
meeting with the team, liaising with management, sorting out
logistics, reviewing my notes, presenting. But there are pauses –
odd moments when I'm alone in an airport or my hotel room and
not completely focused on what needs to be done next. In these
gaps there is none of the normal rhythmic "to-do list" of life
to distract me, no grocery shopping, laundry, cooking, ringing
people. There is no buffer between me and my thoughts.

Dinner in Ghana that night was one of those pauses. For one
hour I deliberately relaxed into the echo of the day, inhabited the
weary intoxication of knowing that one hurdle had been crossed,
and refused to think about the next three days.

I sat by myself at a table outside while the waiter cleared
away all the other place settings, as if to emphasize my
solitude. I used to hate this practice. Now I'm so accustomed to
eating alone that I rarely notice, but that night I thought of my
California friends and smiled. I don't think that being served

fresh fish poolside is what most of them imagine I spend my time in Africa doing. More like risking food poisoning, or worse.

Food poisoning. Not an experience that needed repeating. I made a mental note not to eat the salad that would come with dinner. That was where the biggest risk would lie.

Dinner. Malaria medication needed to be taken with dinner. I dug through my bag for the pills, only then thinking that maybe I should have chosen to sit inside instead of braving the mosquitoes.

The soft darkness and winsome breeze were too beautiful. I decided not to move.

At the next table a French couple united against the pleas of their young son, who had returned from the buffet with three deserts. Implacable, they sent back the crème caramel and the boy began to cry. I learned that the romance of the language does have its limits; a child whining in French is no more charming than one whining in English.

I opened the book I was holding and focused on a quote by Marcel Proust.

"Come now! Were everything clear to you all would seem in vain. Your boredom would populate a shadowless universe with an impassive life made up of unleavened souls. But a measure of disquiet is a divine gift. The hope which, in your eyes, shines on a dark threshold does not have its basis in an overly certain world."

Would a shadowless universe really not be preferable if it meant finally, permanently, illuminating the darkness?

I have often seen refugees in airports in Africa on their way to their new lives, holding nothing but sleeping children and sealed plastic bags full of official documents. I examine them covertly while we all wait to board, trying to imagine what it is like to leave behind the only home you have ever known, perhaps forever, on the strength of nothing but the uncertain hope that there *must* be something better across that wide, dark oceanic threshold.

Caught in the departure lounge, in that final pause separating a grim past and the unknown, I can rarely discern either disquiet or hope in their eyes.

Just exhaustion.

Five men strutted across the lobby of the hotel and pushed through the glass doors toward us, commandeering the last remaining table by the pool. They were tall and lithe, moved with authority, even gestured loudly. Three of them wore white tunics that dropped from neck to ankle, magnificent against skin that was darker than the night sky.

They ignored the crying child but spared me a little more attention without noticeable pause in their animated debate about the credibility of someone I eventually surmised was a local politician, or maybe a gangster.

I returned my eyes to the book and William Inge spoke.

"He who will live for others will have great troubles, but they shall seem to him small. He who will live for himself shall have small troubles, but they shall seem to him great."

What does it really mean, to live for others? Does motive or action take the lead in that tango?

People often ask me what I do, and if I describe it just right I can come off sounding like a cross between Indiana Jones and Florence Nightingale.

"Wow," one woman said to me recently, "that's not a job, that's a calling."

Yes, in some ways. But I have often wondered whether it's not an inferior high-adrenaline substitute for the living for others that happens day after day in marriage and parenthood. The kind of living for others that slowly wears the sharp edges off your core selfishness, that plays out in a million little installments instead of the occasional big sacrifice.

I'm pretty sure it's easier to live for others when they are half a world away and you just visit occasionally.

Music drifted out over the pale marble tiles that circled the pool. *Nothing's gonna change my love...Cherish...Wind beneath my wings... I can't live if living is without you.* It was the same type of music, I suddenly realized, that I'd heard at the airport, on the radio in every taxi, and in the hotel lobby competing valiantly with the soccer commentary: '80s love songs.

I looked at the empty chair opposite me and thought about feeling lonely, but I was too tired. I settled for wistful.

I wondered what my family was doing right then. Where was Mike? Was he thinking of me, or had he mostly thought the better of our sudden e-friendship? Was he eating alone and feeling far from home?

Home.

All those places that I lived growing up did feel at least somewhat like home during the time we lived there. That had something to do with the little things we took with us, those portable threads of continuity: books, music, and pictures. But it had more to do with people. With family – those other four who were always there – and with friends. Without those people somewhere in the picture, there was no amount of "stuff" that could make a place even come close to feeling like home.

I laid my book aside as the food arrived and let my thoughts slide past the next three weeks and settle back in California. In three weeks I would be the one laughing with friends over dinner. Perhaps someone else would sit alone across the room, a silent witness to our camaraderie, savoring their moment of anonymous solitude and thinking that for them, too, home rests far more on the foundation of people than of place.

Perhaps they would remember that we all stand shadowless and disconnected from substance and meaning unless illuminated by the care and insight of others. And that while we may need pauses to recharge, life is lived in communion.

Perhaps they would also think about place and people like this and then wonder why the puzzle of home still did not feel complete and what the missing pieces were.

Los Angeles – Accra – **Washington, D.C.** – Sydney – Zagreb – South Bend – Nairobi – San Diego – Atlanta – Madang – Kona – Canberra – **London** – **Baltimore** – **Itonga** – Vancouver – Harare – Dushanbe – Lira – Petats – Port Moresby – Brisbane – Ballina – Malibu

ICICLES IN HEATHROW

London, UK

A WEEK LATER I walked into Heathrow Airport. The icicles decorating it were a sudden and disconcerting reminder that Christmas was coming.

When I had transited through Heathrow two weeks earlier on my way to Nairobi, there had been no streamers of blue light cascading from the ceiling or coned evergreens winking fiercely. Now there were. Starbucks had not been selling coffee in red and white cardboard cups and drawing Santa hats and candy canes on its chalkboards. Now it was.

I sat in my favorite airport café, Pret a Porter, and tried to take stock. The abrupt realization that Christmas season had arrived in the West while I had been gone was jarring, and the pink pigs hanging from the roof of the next store and whizzing in battery-powered circles didn't exactly prove grounding. I got up, ditched my coffee cup, and prepared to waste the next several hours of my life wandering through airport limbo.

Twelve hours from then, I knew, I'd be landing in Washington, D.C. Michelle would want to know how the trip had been. And I wouldn't know where to start, because the previous two weeks had been more a stream of potent, rushing moments than a story.

Saturday, the day before I leave Los Angeles. I am dressed in my pajamas at a costume party and sitting outside on the cold stone bench of a barbecue eating Mexican food without the safety net of a paper plate.

Two days later, Monday, a twenty-four-hour layover in London. I am sitting on a gravestone and eating meat pies, again with no safety net in sight. A friend from high school, Angela, and I did try to find a bench, but they were all full of uniformed British schoolchildren who for some reason were not in school, so we figured that the occupant of this particular grave would not mind the company. We talk of friends we knew when we were both teenagers growing up in a peaceful, promising Zimbabwe that no longer exists. We watch Angie's toddler, Abby, sleep in her pram. She is a stark reminder of the fact, bewildering to me, that we are no longer teenagers. How did that happen?

Thursday. Nairobi. Work. During workshops I am nowhere else. There are only words and thoughts, and I am always searching for the right questions. One day of facilitating drains three days' worth of energy. I work again over solitary dinners by the pool, occasionally glancing up to see bougainvillea glowing purple in the shadows. A waiter, a beautiful man – tall and graceful and dressed in a spotless tuxedo – thoughtfully carries over a glowing copper brazier and places it near me to ward off the dark's chill. We share a silent smile. I go back to work.

Wednesday. Accra. The last workshop is over. The bubble of total absorption breaks and Ghana elbows its way in.

It's 6 a.m. and I'm headed north on my last day in the country with a silent driver named George for one precious day of adventuring.

Traffic and people. Chaos and heat. Pollution and dust glued to me in equal measure by the humidity. Women balancing buckets and boxes on their heads, selling plantains car to car.

10 a.m., Elmina castle – the Portuguese and Dutch trading post that brokered the most valuable of commodities, slaves, until the late 1800s. I am standing on the governor's balcony overlooking the three stone cells that used to hold hundreds of female slaves awaiting the transport ships. At the governor's pleasure, the women would be driven from these holding pens into the courtyard below to mill around until he had made his daily choice.

When I look up I can see a church in the middle of the castle, placed directly over the dungeons that used to hold male slaves. In that church, words from Psalms 132:14 are inscribed above the door: "This is my resting place forever; Here I will dwell, for I have desired it."

I stare at it and want to cry with rage and shame. And fear. What modern blind spots or willful, apathetic ignorance of ours will goad future generations into similar paroxysms?

I don't cry, though. I am not very good at crying. Outwardly, anyway.

1 p.m. More than one hundred feet up, standing on planks and holding on to ropes, I look down into the treetops of Kakum national park and watch butterflies waft through the rain-forest canopy. There is a tiny, brilliant gecko by my sneaker – an emerald on legs.

4 p.m., Tetteh Quashi market. I buy an oil painting on rice-

sack canvas that I do not need because I see the talent of the
artist, and his pride mixed with anger, and I wonder what I would
sell if my lot were a market stall on a dusty corner.

11 p.m., Kotoka Airport, in Accra. The blank, endured space
of the crowded gate lounge on a hot African night. On the plane
I resent the roundness of the man beside me, the touch this
compels, but refuse to relinquish the armrest completely.

When I was twenty-one I spent three weeks traveling around
New Zealand and there's a moment from that trip I sometimes
think of in the midst of all the moments of these trips. I was in
an inflatable raft, shivering in a wet suit, about to plunge over
the highest commercially raftable waterfall in the world. We
got snagged for a moment at the top of the fall and there was
a deliciously terrifying, wonderfully focusing pause before we
teetered on the very edge of that 21-foot drop. Then the raft went
completely vertical and folded in on itself. Mashed against the
others, blind, I opened my mouth to scream and was invaded
by the ocean of water that had followed us over. The pressure
was unbearable. Then, suddenly, it was over. We popped out
the bottom, the raft unfolded the right way up in the calm of the
eddy and most of us were even still in it – torn between shrieks
of fear, laughter, and a silent awe that we were still alive.

We navigated seventeen sets of rapids that day in New
Zealand, and that's what these work trips sometimes feel like. To
adapt a metaphor from Anais Nin – like living for weeks in the
rapids where novels are born but not written.

Today. Friday. London. As I step out of the plane it's
suddenly freezing and I am adrift, caught in this enforced eddy.

I look around in the sudden stillness and realize.

The raft is still the right way up.

There are blue icicles hanging from the ceiling in Heathrow.
And Christmas is coming.

Washington, D.C., USA

I SPENT MOST OF the next week in the basement of my sister's house, dressed in her flannel pajamas and working on a big report on staff care for humanitarian workers in Sudan and Chad. It was a good place to be buried in a huge project, for on those occasions when I did come up for air there was Thanksgiving with family, my young niece to smile at, the fanciest automatic coffee maker I'd ever seen, and Michelle to chat with.

"Wow," Michelle said one night when I ventured up to the kitchen in search of ice cream. "You *do* have to work hard for your job sometimes."

"What do you mean?" I said, digging through her freezer. "Do you have any chocolate mint?"

"There are already four different types in there," Michelle said. "You'll just have to make do with one of those."

"I work hard," I said, returning to her previous comment and resigning myself to plain old chocolate.

"It's just that most times we chat on the phone," Michelle said, "it's just after five in L.A. and you've already left the office."

"That is not called 'not working'," I said. "That is called good work-life balance."

I looked down. It was after eight at night. I had not changed out of pajamas that day, or showered. I had two more sections to write before I could go to bed.

"That balance sometimes vanishes when I'm on the road," I said. "This project is a disaster and we'll be lucky to get it finished before I have to leave to run the Baltimore symposium."

"Oh, so you *are* still working now. I thought maybe you were down there writing emails to that guy. ... What's his name?"

"Oh, uh, Mike, you mean," I said.

"How's that going?" Michelle asked when I didn't supply any more details.

"First," I said, pointing a recently emptied spoon at her, "there is no 'that.' We are just getting to know one another as friends. Second, I don't know. He's on some island somewhere and has been for more than two weeks. I won't hear from him until he returns to civilization."

Michelle didn't push me any harder that night and I was grateful, for the truth of the matter was that I *was* interested on some level. As careful as I had been to lay down boundaries in those first emails to Mike and to never allow myself to indulge in that naughty art of e-flirtation in any of my letters since, I had already caught myself wondering more than once whether maybe, just maybe, Mike and I might have a real shot at something more than friendship. I didn't want to try to explain that even to Michelle, for Michelle had had a front-row seat the last time I'd tried long-distance love and *that* show had been anything but pretty. I doubted that she would bring the past up and lecture me, but I wasn't taking any chances. I didn't need to, I told myself. I'd learned my lessons well with regard to long-distance relationships. These lessons were, in fact, remarkably similar to the rules that lifeguards at public pools used to drill into us over and over on steamy summer days.

Danger!

Walk, don't run, because the ground here is slippery.

And no diving in headfirst, even if the water *looks* like it might be deep enough.

Baltimore, USA

INQUIRIES INTO MY LOVE life were, it seemed, once again

the flavor of the month. The next conversation on this topic came just three days later, in Baltimore.

It had finally stopped raining, although the pavement was still wet and the streets steaming in protest against the November chill. I was in my own little world, juggling my laptop and bag, when I stepped onto the curb near my hotel and he spoke to me.

"Did you get your coffee?" he asked. "*Oy vay*, you look tired."

"I am tired," I said, recognizing the smiling, bowler-hatted limousine driver who had introduced himself as Gideon and pointed out the coffee shop to me that morning. "I've been thinking for five hours. My brain hurts."

"It's cold, ey?" he said. "Where I'm from in Africa it isn't this cold."

"No," I said, remembering the heat that had chased me onto the plane ten days earlier. "I know, I was in Africa last week."

"Where?"

"Kenya and Ghana."

"Oh," he said, disappointed. "Not Nigeria? You should go to Nigeria. It is the best place. Why have you not married an African man?"

I did a double take. Nope, we were definitely standing on a street corner in Baltimore. And, yes, I was discussing this topic with a total stranger for the second time in three weeks.

About three weeks earlier I had been in a taxi in Nairobi. It was a Jatco taxi, Jatco being one of the handful of taxi companies in Nairobi where you can be reasonably sure you won't be robbed mid-journey – not by the taxi driver, anyway. This safe-service guarantee apparently doesn't, however, extend to protection from being propositioned.

I was staring out the window, exhausted after a long day of facilitating, when the taxi driver, who was blessed with the unlikely name of Bunny, spoke into the silence.

"Are you married?"

I sighed. I knew we still had about forty minutes of traffic on Muta Gisau Way to contend with. It was going to be a long trip back to the hotel.

"No."

"Ah, I think you must marry an African man," Bunny said.

"Why?"

"Ahhhh. African man is very good. Very hard-working. But I think maybe you best should pick an African man with no money. That is very good."

At this I was curious beyond all restraint.

"Why?"

"When man have no money and woman have a little money, then they come together," Bunny brought both hands together to illustrate this important point, thereby taking them off the wheel and almost running us into the back of a minivan in the process. "Then they work together to make *lots* of money."

"Plus," Bunny added as the coup de grace, "man with no money will be more faithful than man with lots of money."

"Huh."

"How old are you?" Bunny asked.

"Thirty one," I said.

Bunny clearly knew something about Western women. Usually when I gave this answer, I got a look that hovered between shock and concern and sometimes an interrogation into how and why I had managed to reach this age unwed. Was my father negligent? How high, exactly, was my bride price?

But Bunny shot me a winsome smile. "Ahhh! You are very young. You are too young! Do you like African men?"

"I like Africa. I like coming to Kenya."

"That is good. I myself am in the marriage process. Yes," he said.

Temporarily relieved, thinking there was a girlfriend on the scene, I ventured actively into the conversation.

"Oh, are you engaged?" I asked.

"Not yet. But soon."

"Oh, do you have a girlfriend?"

"Oh, no. Not yet. But soon. I am liking the white woman."

By this stage I figured that all hope of a graceful and reserved exit from this taxi had completely disappeared and I might as well ask the question on my mind.

"What is so good about white women?"

"Ahhh ... They are very good at the love."

This was more of an answer than I had bargained for. Thankfully I stayed quiet long enough for Bunny to speak again. "They are very good at the relationship. They have lots of understanding."

"Understanding of what?" I asked, confused. "Politics?"

Bunny laughed at me. "They are very social."

It *was* a long trip back to my hotel, albeit a rather entertaining one. By the end of it, Bunny had figured out that I probably wasn't keen on marrying him. That didn't stop him from handing me his phone number and email address as I got out.

"Do you think it's possible," he asked, "that we could meet?"

At least I think he said *meet*. It might have been *mate*—the way his accent, with its beautiful round cadence, smoothed out the words made it hard for me to tell, but I chose to give him the benefit of the doubt. The answer was the same in any case.

"I don't think it is possible," I said.

At this Bunny gave me one last grin. "Ahhh, but with God all things are possible."

Bunny definitely had the last word in that conversation. I

had to agree that, yes, with God all things are possible, but I still wasn't going to meet, or mate.

But between Bunny in Kenya and now Gideon in Baltimore, I was beginning to wonder if I just might be missing something. After all, I sometimes thought, I'd made several other major life decisions on the basis of reasoning that more than one small nudge in the direction of an open door was irrefutable proof, quite possibly divine guidance, that I should walk through that door. Many of those decisions had worked out all right. Perhaps I was making a mistake by continuing to turn down these types of offers, offers that never seemed to come from remotely sensible options who actually lived anywhere near L.A.

As we shook farewell, Gideon held my hand a shade longer than necessary.

"If you have spent time in Africa, then you know me, here," Gideon said, placing his hand over his heart. "And since I have lived here for almost ten years now, there is not so much I don't know about you, I think. That makes love not so hard, I think."

I smiled, thinking that I seemed to learn more about love every time I talked to a taxi driver.

"Give me a call at your convenience," Gideon said, handing me his card. "I'll take you to Nigeria."

Itonga, Vanuatu

WHILE I WAS EATING chocolate ice cream out of the carton and chatting to taxi drivers on street corners, it seemed that Mike had been very far from both ice cream and street corners. When a flurry of emails from him hit my inbox after three weeks of silence, I smiled and immediately settled in to read the first of these, a mass email to friends and family about his time in Vanuatu.

Monday, November 26
From: Mike Wolfe
To: Friends
Subject: White skin and other tales from the bush

"If our blood is the same color, why is my skin black and your skin white?" the village chief asked me. It was my second day in Itonga village on Tanna Island. Relative to the nearest skyscraper, Itonga is a four-hour flight, then a one-hour hop in an eight-seater biplane, then an hour drive down rutted dirt roads, then a thirty-minute walk down into a tropical ravine on a steep path crowded by dense foliage. No cars, no computers, no mobile phones, no light bulbs, no Coca-Cola (gasp).

There's a beautiful simplicity to life in the bush. The taro roots (breakfast, lunch, dinner) come straight from the rich dark volcanic soil of hillside gardens. Coconuts grow all around. The meat is slaughtered just hours or minutes before we eat it, the muscles still twitching as three men pick up an entire side of the cow and carry it to the roasting pit. The water comes from the creek, which is nourished in turn by the downpours and the gentle, steady rains that drip down thousands of verdant green leaves.

In the evenings, men sit under the magnificent banyan tree drinking kava and telling stories while the women finish up the day's work, sometimes with a chorus of voices singing thanks to God. Sunrise, sunset. Simple. Sitting in Itonga on my last day of three weeks of the bush, as the gentle rains massaged the bamboo hut, I felt an amazing sense of connectedness. It was a beautiful moment. Pity that it took me three weeks to arrive at that moment. For up until my last day in the bush, I had been mostly counting the days until I got to leave.

I've been doing this humanitarian aid and development work for a few years now. I still struggle with my white skin. Most of the time it's a liability, I think. When I show up in a village people think "Father Christmas," which is in direct opposition to what we're aiming to do. We're trying to help the community see ways that they can improve their sanitation and hygiene practices themselves instead of just waiting for handouts from others, which is essentially what they've been conditioned to expect from centuries of village strongmen, colonialists, missionaries, and consultants. I loathe the extra attention I get in these villages and I go out of my way to keep a low profile. During our sessions with the community, longing to go completely unnoticed, I try to sit at the back of the meeting place. But alas, despite my best efforts, there are rarely other white people in these villages and I can't just blend in. Goodbye anonymity, hello foreign zoo animal on display for all curious onlookers.

So during the past few weeks a lot of the thoughts that have sprung to mind have had something to do with looking forward to getting back to "civilization." Cold beer, red wine, chocolate, hot shower, comfortable bed, food that makes my taste buds dance (taro three times a day gets old pretty quickly). Not having to watch people sit around picking lice out of each other's hair. Yep.

And clattering around in my head have also been anxious thoughts about what I'm going to do next, and whether I can actually go on much longer in this exciting/ exhausting line of work. My first contract here finishes in three months. I feel pulled to leave the field and settle down in America, where certainly things would be more normal and where my white skin wouldn't stand out. But I also I feel drawn to living in the field closer to the communities where there are real needs. And I'd like to actually live and work in the same place for more than one year.

And so early in the mornings while I'm walking down the well-trodden path to the river to bathe, these thoughts bombard me. Certainly it must be better living back in America. Certainly I'd be able to find a normal job, and I'd be able to surround myself with good friends, and I could adjust to living in a world with broadband. And I'd be anonymous. I could just be a normal person again.

And of course there would be no rush-hour traffic, no moments of loneliness, no information overload from having to select one of 45 different calling plans from mobile phone providers, and no frustrations with insurance companies, and no strain from 24-hour news updates. Yes, life back in America would certainly be bliss.

So walking back from the river after bathing, or in between planning sessions with the communities, the question that has continued to surface in my mind during the past three weeks: Why do I continue to choose to live and work in places where I'm always an outsider to some extent, where isolation and loneliness are reliable companions?

Well, after three weeks in the bush, here it is: despite all the painful and uncomfortable moments, I still feel drawn to do it. I still have desire to use my abilities to help others. I still believe that people are valuable. And occasionally, just occasionally, I get to catch a glimpse of the difference that my work can make in the lives of people who are living in some pretty difficult circumstances. There's still great purpose in this work, and at least for now I still believe the most effective role I can play in it all is to be the engineer who spends three weeks in the bush training national staff how to conduct sessions on community planning and design effective water and sanitation systems.

> *So I vacillate between wanting to pack up all my stuff
> and get on the next plane home and wanting to get on the back
> of a pickup truck heading out to the bush. But right now, despite
> the restlessness, the continual pondering opportunity cost,
> the complexities of being a foreigner, the power dynamics of
> development work, and the yearning for the normal, it's worth it.*
>
> *"Your skin is black and my skin is white," I told the chief
> in my best broken Bislama, "because in America the sun is cold.
> In Vanuatu the sun is very hot."*
>
> *He was satisfied with my answer. So am I.*

> *P.S. As I was leaving Itonga, the chief gave me a traditional
> bow and arrow and a woven basket. Gender roles being what
> they are in the Pacific, the chief explained to me that the man
> hunts and the woman follows with the basket tied across her
> head to gather what the man kills. So now I have my bow
> and arrow, and a basket. Which is going to be more difficult:
> successfully killing the prey or finding the woman to follow after
> me and pick up the kill? In my first try with the bow, I managed
> to miss a target that was only five meters away.*

Mike, Papua New Guinea

SENT WITH THIS LETTER was another, more personal one to
me alone.

"It rained for almost 36 hours straight, so when we left the
village yesterday the small trickling creek at the bottom of the
ravine had been transformed into a muddy torrent," Mike began.
"We had to wade through waist-high brown water to get out of
the village. But I am back from the bush now, and thank God for
hot showers and razors and beer. Aaahhh."

He was enjoying local Thai food and a cold beer, he wrote. He'd also just enjoyed a couple of days off work to do some world-class scuba diving and "caving, climbing across boulders, swimming down a canyon, jumping off rocks, and all sorts of little boy adventures."

As we had signed off three weeks earlier, I had told him that when we were both back on terra firma I would want to know, in detail, about three highs and three lows of his time away. That's what filled the rest of this second letter – several thousand words on brilliant, sunset-lighted highs and some searing lows.

He finished with a bit of teasing and a few questions.

"I read the taxi driver essay you sent out," Mike wrote. "I laughed, although I'm actually quite jealous because I've never been able to manage to get a proposition from an African man. So if/when I leave the field and move back to the 'normal' world, does that mean that I'll still receive multiple offers to marry the daughter of whatever village I happen to visit? And speaking of normal, is it normal for those of us at this 30s stage of life to be constantly pondering whether we're better off spreading our wings and pursuing our dreams of careers with adventure and excitement and purpose or whether we're better off going 'home' (wherever that is) and doing something 'normal' (whatever that is) and having stable friendships and singing kumbaya at night?

"Your writings are funny. And vulnerable. I know you said that you read essays like that so many times before you send them that they don't seem so vulnerable, but you do really bare yourself. I like it. It's genuine. Naked. But why *do* you choose to write essays and post them online for all the digitally connected world to peruse?"

Lisa, USA

"I REALLY ENJOYED READING your white skin essay,"
I began my own letter back to him later that night, cushioned
against the cold by the fluffy white comforters adorning the hotel
bed, my laptop on my lap. "But regardless of whether we blend
in on the outside we'll never be internally anonymous again,
you know. We've both passed that point of no return where we
could ever fit into one 'place' completely again – either here or
there. I'm not sad about that, except very occasionally when I'm
having a really bad day and being entirely unreasonable. But
it does regularly make things less than comfortable on a non-
abstract basis. That constant restiveness can seem more like a
curse or a goad than a blessing a lot of the time. Where does that
restiveness come from?

"I think it comes from having seen a lot. Knowing that the
world is my oyster at this stage and that choices (well, more than
one, or two, or ten) are mine for the making about what I want to
do and where I want to be. And an internal and unwinnable war
between my need for intensity/novelty/challenge and my deep
longing for routine/comfort/a normal.

"As for chiefs' daughters, this is something that I can speak
with authority on. You will still receive multiple offers to marry
chiefs' daughters when you visit villages after leaving the field
– probably even more of them since your stock will have risen,
as you are no longer crazy enough to actually be living in their
country but are living in the land of plenty, where everyone else
wants to live.

"And why do I write essays and put them online? The real
reason why I wrote my very first essay? Sad to say it wasn't
uncontrollable artistic urges or existential angst desperate for
outlet or anything similarly noble-sounding. Really, when it

came right down to it, my primary motivation for writing my first essay was to catch someone's attention. Yes, translate that to: to impress a guy."

I stopped typing.

Mike's questions were pointing me toward my past. Toward murky territory I hadn't revisited for more than a year. Toward one story I *hadn't* written about and posted on the www for all the digitally connected world to peruse.

"You know Ryan Schmidt?" I had carefully asked Mike in one of our earliest emails after we discovered all our mutual acquaintances. "I tracked Ryan down very similarly to the way you just tracked me down – through an essay of his that a friend of a friend forwarded to me."

Just how much more of this tale was I willing to share with a distant, familiar stranger?

Los Angeles – Accra – Washington, D.C. – Sydney – Zagreb – South Bend – Nairobi – San Diego – Atlanta – Madang – Kona – Canberra – London – **Baltimore** – Itonga – **Vancouver** – Harare – Dushanbe – Lira – Petats – Port Moresby – Brisbane – Ballina – Malibu

CHASING SILVER DOLLARS

Los Angeles, USA

A COMPLETE ANSWER TO Mike's question about why I write essays would have started the story more than three years earlier. Shortly after I moved to L.A., a friend forwarded me an essay she had stumbled across and enjoyed, an essay written by a Canadian named Ryan who was living in Afghanistan.

"I turned thirty in Afghanistan," Ryan's essay began. "It was my second birthday here. Last year I was hit with a weird flu three days before and the fever finally broke as I entered the last year of my twenties. My friend, Halim, came into my room to my weak groans and cheerily offered me a bowl of rice and beans. He told me again that no doubt I had malaria. 'Today check blood?' he asked hopefully, just like every other day. Here everything is malaria. If you have a toothache they suspect malaria."

It was a short essay, barely a thousand words, but it inspired the first truly electric flicker of interest I'd felt since the heartbreak of Notre Dame. After I finished reading the piece, I forwarded it on to my parents with a brief and blithe "Read this. It's amazing. I'm going to track him down and make him fall in love with me."

But Ryan turned out to be harder to track down than I'd expected. I didn't have a last name or an email address. I had to trace the trail back through my friend to her brother, who also lived in Afghanistan, to a friend of Ryan's in Canada who sent out Ryan's essays and compiled any replies into one document for him, a system prompted by internet constraints in the remote province where Ryan was based.

Ryan's friend cheerfully agreed to add me to the distribution list, so I settled in to wait for the next installment. When it came, the essay, titled *A Portable Life*, cut to my core.

"I crave Adventure," Ryan wrote. "Sometimes I flip through my passport just to feel the 48 pages of possibilities. But I'm also completely obsessed with the idea of Home."

> It's really something to travel the world, to bump over roads in Russian jeeps, to see the villages, the citadels, the minarets, the mosques, but it's not the same without the memory of Vancouver back home. It's beautiful to fly in over Vancouver on a summer evening and see the Lion's Gate lit up like a drawbridge on a fairy castle, but it's only if I've been away on the dusty roads that I get that feeling of my heart collapsing in relief like a knight at the end of a long battle. As exciting as adventures are, there's too little of home in any of them. And even though there's no place like home,

there's not much adventure there.

The fact is, I feel a bit restless no matter where I am. The more world I see the more it delights me, terrifies me, astounds me, and the more I become convinced that it will never be the right world for me. Maybe somewhere in me is a distant memory of a world from my childhood or even before that, from the time I was a twinkle in Abraham's sky, from the moment the voice spoke into the darkness and light rose like a daisy.

I'm not ungrateful; I love it here, maybe even more for all the longing. But there is neither home nor adventure enough for me in this world. What there is is enough of each to set me off questing for a place where home is really Home and adventure is really Adventure – enough to satisfy the paradoxical longings of my soul.

It might not even be a place or a thing that I want. There's a part in one of Frederick Buechner's novels that I love. A man has a dream that he finds a silver dollar with a name on it. He says,

"It wasn't any of the other names I've been called by various people at various times in my life, and yet it was my name. It was a name so secret that I wouldn't tell it even if I remembered it, and I don't remember it. But if anybody were ever to show up and call me by it I'd recognize it in a second, and the chances are that if the person who called me by it gave me the signal, I'd follow him to the ends of the earth."

I wonder if that's just it. Suppose what I keep calling home and adventure could do with a bigger name, say, "God." Suppose when God says, "Come on, let's go home," or, "Follow me on this adventure" – suppose it's all the same thing, simply because God is there.

What if with God there is enough adventure at home and enough home in the adventure?

I don't just need a better world, I need a better self; I need a real name. The backpacks and the down jacket and the computer I've selected so carefully as the building blocks of my portable life are a poor substitute at best. But one day I believe that Someone will come and flip me my silver dollar and call my name. Then I'll drop these three bags in the twinkling of an eye and discover the real world at last.

I sat there breathless and stunned for a long time after finishing Ryan's essay. Then I had only one real question.

How *was* I going to connect with this mysterious man who wrestled with questions of home and adventure the way I did, who had named my struggles and who seemed a lot more hopeful than I was at that point that there may somewhere, somehow, someday be reconciliation of those contradictory longings for adventure and for home?

This was the question I pondered during the next two weeks while I packed up my own portable life and hopped on a plane for the first of what would be many trips to Kenya for work.

It was a tough assignment, and to top it all off I came down with a terrible case of what I finally figured out was food poisoning. By the time I arrived back in L.A., I'd lost eight pounds, hadn't eaten much more than yogurt and apple juice in a week, and I had my answer. Ryan's raw, lyrical honesty had shivered through me on some deep level – as if he'd struck a large bronze bell in my soul. Perhaps my own honesty would evoke a similar resonance.

So that is when I sat down and wrote my first essay, all about that first trip to Kenya, and sent it out into the universe and to

Ryan.

———— ⚬⚬⚬ ————

TO BE HONEST, I was rather unreasonably confident when I sent out this essay that it would evoke *some* response from Ryan. So I was more than a little surprised and disappointed when the days, then weeks, passed with no reply.

But then I got distracted.

The same week I sent out the essay about Kenya, I received an email from Colorado. From someone who was *not* on my mailing list. From someone whom I had been matched with five months earlier when (bored and lonely right after my move to L.A.) I'd been dabbling in online dating.

Jason lived in Colorado and worked for a publishing company. When we were first matched up online I had thought he sounded promising, but before we ever got beyond a couple of emails he forthrightly let me know that he'd decided to pursue another match who also lived in Denver.

Then, after months of silence, I heard from him again.

The woman in Denver hadn't worked out, he said. He'd been thinking about me and wondering how I was. Would I like to chat sometime?

"Sure," I thought. "Why not? What did I have to lose?"

Soon Jason and I were talking on the phone every day.

My initial instincts had been right: there was promise here. He was warm, sweet, and transparent. He asked a lot of great questions. He paid close attention to the answers. And four weeks after we started talking long distance we were practically dating.

We made plans for him to come and visit me in California in the beginning of September.

And then Ryan wrote to me.

He'd just finished a month-long assignment and was headed back to Canada. He'd been catching up on email at Heathrow Airport. He'd read my essay.

"I don't know you," he said, "but you're up my alley. If you ever find yourself in Vancouver, sing Australian drinking songs on a corner until someone flips you two bits from pity, then call me."

Then he gave me his phone number.

It is at this point that I started to get very, very confused.

BEFORE LONG I FOUND myself emailing Ryan many mornings and talking to Jason for hours on the phone every night. I still hadn't met either one of these guys in person – I hadn't even talked to Ryan or seen a photo of him – so I couldn't exactly figure out why I was starting to feel like the worst sort of cheater.

But I was. And it was catapulting me back in time a dozen years. To the tainted era of my first kisses.

Technically, I guess, the kiss I'm thinking of wasn't my first. But if you don't count the quick peck executed in front of ten pairs of thrilled eyes during a game of truth or dare when I was in fifth grade, then my first kiss was with my first boyfriend, Dion.

I was sixteen and Dion was a kingly two years older. I was in Zimbabwe at the time, attending an all-girls school. Dion was the head boy of our brother school. He attended my church and I'd watched him, interested and somewhat awed, for months. Interested because he just seemed so … nice. Awed because, in the rigid and hierarchical British school system, the prefects were a remote and authoritative sort of royalty. And so, for the first three months of that year, whenever I was bored in church, I just watched.

I did a lot of watching.

But I didn't do anything else until the date of the fourth-form ball began to loom.

I didn't want to go to this dance. Spending my teenage years in Zimbabwe had been good for a great many things. I had, for example, learned how to sew baby clothes on a hand-crank sewing machine, ride a horse, use a log table instead of a calculator, make bread from scratch, and locate a cattle dip tank on a topographical map. What I had not done was learn how to dance.

(I had not learned any algebra either, but that wouldn't come back to haunt me for another year, until after we'd relocated back to the U.S.)

So, dancing.

I'd already suffered through a couple of school dances in preceding years, and they'd been truly painful. At fourteen I was fascinated by the boys, these creatures we never saw during school hours who just appeared, so neatly groomed, at the chaperoned events in the school hall. I longed to be asked to dance and I was terrified of being asked to dance. More than once I panicked and made a quick escape to the bathroom when it looked as if a boy was approaching with intent. Then I would stay there, locked in a stall, until I figured the coast was clear.

I wasn't at all sure I wanted to go to my own fourth-form ball – a formal affair to which we were expected to bring *an actual date* – but my girlfriends begged and harassed and teased until we struck a deal.

"Okay," I said. "I'll ask one guy. If he says yes, I'll come. If he says no, I am off the hook."

We all agreed that this was fair. So I went to church the next week, sucked in a deep breath, and went up and asked Dion.

He said yes.

I had such a glorious time that night. Not even the memory of the dress I'd had custom-made for the occasion (a bright pink satin frock overlaid with black organza and sporting a big bow on the back) can erase my smile when I stop to think about that first taste of the surety of being partnered and the exhilaration of finally relinquishing self-consciousness on the dance floor.

Dion did not kiss me that night. In fact, he didn't kiss me until we were well into the six months we spent as an official couple after attending the ball. And even then I never really felt it counted because he never kissed me *with tongue*.

Dion was every bit as nice as I'd judged him to be, the sort of considerate and respectful first boyfriend parents dream about for their daughters. In addition to being the high school equivalent of the president, he ran track, he played in a local Christian rock band, he even wrote me a song. But to his credit and my great disappointment, what he never did was put his tongue in my mouth or his hands anywhere he would have been embarrassed for our pastor to see them.

When he broke up with me after six chaste months, he told me it was because he felt as if he were dating his sister.

"Perhaps," I thought resentfully, "if you'd kissed me with tongue I might have felt a little less like your sister."

WHEN DION BROKE UP with me I was determined not to turn seventeen without having experienced *real kissing*. In retrospect, this is perhaps one of the clearest examples of my ability to resolutely and willfully pursue experience for experience's sake – an ability that has not always served me well.

The person who served me up my first "real kiss" was the friend of a friend. We were out together, part of a larger group on a Friday night. We'd gone to the one movie theater in town and then back to someone's house to watch another movie. We sat at the back of the room together, cuddled under a blanket. I had heard he had a girlfriend, but I kissed him anyway. If he wasn't going to say anything about her, why should I?

He tasted like potato chips. His stubble hurt my chin. It was slimy and not all that much fun.

I never saw him again after that night.

I can't remember his name now, but I can remember his girlfriend's name. And I can remember how I felt even before I learned her identity and realized that she was a friendly acquaintance from school.

Dishonorable and ashamed.

And twelve years later, finding myself undeniably interested in both Jason and Ryan, I wasn't at all happy to feel the first faint stirrings of these same uncomfortable feelings.

I tried to tell myself that since we hadn't met face-to-face I wasn't really dating Jason yet. Not *really*. So he didn't yet need to know that I was regularly sending emails north, to a man I found curiously intriguing, right? After all, I had lots of friends I regularly emailed.

And Ryan – I was barely getting to know the guy. I didn't owe him full disclosure on other people I talked to, did I?

<hr>

IT WAS JASON I fretted over most.

On the one hand, telling myself that it would be better to wait until after we met before we decided whether to date more seriously was eminently sensible. The only problem with this was that I had *not* thus far been eminently sensible in how I set about getting to know Jason across the miles.

For the first six weeks that Jason and I were talking, my

entire emotional world revolved around our phone calls. Emboldened by the safety of distance and titillated by the mystery that distance enforced, we took the initial spark we had felt and fanned it energetically.

I skated through work, storing up tidbits to share in long, lazy conversations with Jason that night. Nothing I said and no detail he offered me seemed too boring or trivial for us to discuss or laugh over. For the first time in seven long years, I tasted that sweet narcotic of belonging that seems to come only with knowing that you are being treasured and adored by someone else.

We had no idea how the other person moved, smelled, acted around others, or dealt with frustration. We had no sense of what it would be like to look into each other's eyes. But the immediate warmth of our emotional connection over the phone and an untarnished sense of possibility proved giddily intoxicating. With big decisions as far away as across the country and as accessible as the voice in our ear, we mentioned marriage as a possibility before we ever met.

More than once.

I so enjoyed talking to Jason during those early days that it never even occurred to me that it would perhaps be wiser *not* to overdose so eagerly on the emotional intensity we were manufacturing, or to settle too quickly into a pattern of talking every day, or to get into the habit of returning every one of his text messages and calls as soon as humanly possible.

I didn't realize that he would become accustomed to, even dependent on, knowing where I was and what I was doing all the time.

I didn't realize that a couple of months in, when I felt the first stirrings of needing more space and the first flickering of resentment at the enormous amount of time and energy I was devoting to these daily telethons, that I would also find myself feeling totally unable to risk the frustration and disappointment that I feared would come from him if I sought to reshape these communication patterns.

———— ⊗⊗⊗ ————

IN A PLOT TWIST that any good romance novelist would fear being labeled as the banal use of coincidence to conveniently foment drama, Ryan and Jason both wanted to come visit me for the first time on the same weekend.

"Who are you, Lisa McKay?" Ryan wrote to me. "Are you in the habit of writing to strange boys you've never met and inviting them to visit you? If not, why are you inviting me? Because I will come, for some reason. I like your spirit. I like the way you tell your secret doubts and smile. I like that all your words have winks hidden in them. But let's be honest, it would be a bit of a mystery grab-bag of a visit. What if you find me hopelessly boring in person? What if your boyfriend/husband (?) takes exception to you sitting and talking for hours with some boy from the northland?"

"As far as finding you hopelessly boring in person, highly doubtful," I wrote back. "More prosaic than your prose probably. People usually are, in person. If we run into trouble and find ourselves staring at each other over a Starbucks cup looking trapped and thinking, 'Crap! It's only been 20 minutes and we're stuck in this crazy stranger-drama all weekend,' we can always take laptops to the pub and sit and email each other. Then we'd be on firm ground."

And, no, I continued in that email, I wasn't in the habit of inviting strange men to visit me, but while we were on the topic he should know that it just so happened that I'd branched out twice in the last couple of months. Would the weekend *after* Labor Day, when this other guy named Jason was already scheduled to visit me for the first time, suit Ryan just as well?

"I must say I admire your fearlessness," Ryan wrote, "lining up two, um, 'visitors,' one after the other. That, if nothing else, makes you either fascinating or mad, both of which are worth coming to see. I'll be there."

Except … a couple of weeks and more than a few emails later, Ryan had either had second thoughts about that or fate intervened.

His brother needed help moving, Ryan announced unexpectedly via email one day. He had to drive their car across Canada. Could he take a raincheck on coming to Los Angeles?

I was initially gutted, and then relieved, when I got this letter canceling Ryan's visit.

It was all for the best, I told myself. For whenever I wasn't thinking about Ryan, I was happily caught up in the dizzying intensity of my burgeoning whirlwind relationship with Jason, and whatever true fearlessness I possessed had not extended to full disclosure with Jason as I had risked with Ryan.

It wasn't that I didn't *want* to tell Jason. It was just that I was pretty sure that something like "Hey, Jason, I really think I might love you, or that I might come to love you, but there's this other guy I've never met, or even talked to, and there's a very small chance that he *could* just be my soul mate. Can I get back to you on us in two weeks?" would not go down well.

I simply figured that with Ryan having taken himself out of the picture, surely things would get less complicated with Jason.

———✦———

FOR A WHILE – leading up to my first visit with Jason, through the second, and heading towards the third – things *did* get less complicated.

Marginally.

But there was still plenty of complexity to my feelings as I waited at LAX to pick him up for the first time. Sick of pacing, too scared to sit alone with my own thoughts, I called Michelle on my cell phone as I waited.

"Am I crazy?" I asked her.

"Yes," she answered. "But it's a little late to do anything about that now."

I groaned.

"I think I'm going to throw up. Do you think it's too late to leave and just disappear?" I asked.

"Do you *really* want to do that?" Michelle asked.

"No," I finally answered, slowly. "It's just that … I think we may have moved a bit fast."

"How?" Michelle asked. "You haven't even met yet."

"Yes, well … You know how sometimes you say or write things to people when they're not there and you forget that you'll probably actually *see* them someday?"

"Uh," said Michelle, who the year before had married the guy she'd been dating since she was fifteen, "not exactly."

I RANG MICHELLE AGAIN three days later while I was driving home from dropping Jason off at the airport. The weekend had been full of sweet moments and the novel heat of proximity. When I kissed him goodbye at LAX, I promised I'd see him again the following month in Colorado as planned. But I was, if anything, only more confused.

"I had fun, but I really don't know if I can see us together long term," I said.

"Do you think you can figure that out in a single weekend?" Michelle asked.

"No," I finally answered. "That's what dating *is*, right? You spend time with different people until you get sure one way or another."

"Apparently," Michelle said.

There was a brief silence.

I was wondering whether I was even capable of getting sure enough to make that sort of commitment. I wondered whether Michelle was thinking she'd committed too quickly, too young.

"Do you think we might have figured this out earlier if we'd been normal teenagers?" I asked.

"You had boyfriends as a teenager," Michelle said.

"Yeah," I said, "and as far as I know I'm still dating most of them. After Dion I never actually broke up with anyone – I just left the country."

"What about Pete?" Michelle said, naming the last guy I'd dated seriously – Pete and I had made it a whole six whole months when I was a 21-year-old university student.

"Awwww, *Pete*!" I said, smiling at all the good memories. "He was awesome. Technically, though, *he* broke up with me … after I kept talking about how I was planning on leaving the country."

"It is sometimes beyond me," Michelle said, "how you can be a respected expert in stress management.

"That's work," I said. "I'm good at work. This is love."

"I think I should go to Colorado," I said. "Maybe things will become clearer if I see him on his home turf."

"Go to Colorado," Michelle said. "But don't do anything too dumb."

I CAME BACK FROM Colorado excited and exhausted.

"I had a really good time!" I said to Michelle the night I got back.

"Where *are* you?" Michelle asked.

"LAX."

"That's what it sounds like. But didn't you get back this morning?"

"Yeah, I got up at 3 a.m., flew back to L.A. this morning, went home, repacked, and now I'm back. I'm going to South Africa tonight."

"I can't keep up with you," Michelle said. "So what was the weekend like?"

It was really good, I told her. It was fun. His family all seemed lovely. His nephew was adorable. His mother was a great cook. It snowed.

"I haven't heard you say a whole lot about Jason," Michelle said after half an hour. "What are the three things you like most about him?"

"He is very attentive," I said, starting to think out loud. "And he's really good at affirming me."

"What are things that will be there if the attentiveness and affirmation fades?" Michelle asked.

There was a long pause.

"I need time to think about that one, and I've got to go. They're calling boarding. Hey, remember," I said, starting a preflight dialogue we had often, "just in case the plane crashes …"

"I know," Michelle said, finishing the sentence, "you love me."

THERE WERE MOMENTS WHEN I'd see Jason's name on my phone and simply stare at it until it stopped ringing – feeling panicked and trapped, wondering how we'd careened so far down this path of emotional and physical intimacy so rapidly.

There were moments when I buried my face in a bouquet of red roses he'd had delivered to my office, or felt the warm weight of his arms around me during those charged weekend visits, and smiled at the thought of marrying him.

And in the midst of all this confusing and exhilarating sweetness, like a mosquito in my mind, there was still Ryan.

Ryan with whom I was still exchanging sporadic emails. Ryan who represented his own brand of mystery and passion to me. Ryan who, to use his own analogy, seemed to promise a raw, deep adventure to Jason's gentle home.

I knew I wouldn't be able to figure out whether Jason and I really had something unless I threw myself completely into our relationship. But I feared that I might *never* be able to throw myself fully into our relationship and really commit unless I also met someone like Ryan, someone who stood a chance of putting my ideals about a true soul mate to the test.

A soul mate, I believed, would meet me on a visceral, darker level. He would have an instinctive understanding, borne out of experience, of the elements that made up my own particular potpourri of angst – constant change, the guilt of privilege, too much witnessed suffering, a battle between hope and cynicism, and a search for God that wouldn't let you rest even during times when you weren't at all sure you believed in God.

There would be the companionship of keenly felt questions.

Similarly to God, I wasn't at all sure that soul mates actually existed. But, also similarly, I rather hoped they did.

What if this comfortable sweetness I felt with Jason now would someday not be enough? What if my soul mate belonged down the other end of the spectrum, where I had placed Ryan?

There were choices to be made, choices that felt impossible to make in isolation.

"I need to meet both of them," I told Michelle. "If Ryan won't come here, I'm going to Canada."

Michelle had no idea what to say to that one.

My mother, who had also suffered through my narration of this docudrama for months, had no such inhibitions.

"Just *go* already," she said. "It's about time you got yourself sorted out."

IT HAD BEEN SIX months since I was captured so completely by two pages about a stranger's birthday party. Four months since Ryan and I had first exchanged letters. At least three months since I realized that if I didn't meet Ryan I would always wonder. And wondering was the last thing I wanted. I felt torn between what Jason was offering me – marriage, the beauty and safety of a warm and constant affection – and the allure of the challenge and adventure I associated with Ryan.

I had spent more emotional energy on my image of Ryan than had been aroused by some of the people I'd actually dated.

Perhaps if I could put a face to that mystery, I thought, it would throw my feelings for Jason into sharp relief and the way forward would look clearer.

This reasoning felt faulty even as I was formulating it, but I couldn't figure out exactly why. After all, choice is all about contrast, isn't it? How could I figure out if I loved Jason the way he so wanted me to love him, in a vacuum?

But how could I tell Jason now, several months into what was undeniably a serious relationship, that I needed to cross an international border to go on a blind date with a stranger – a stranger, incidentally, who wouldn't exactly *know* he was on a blind date and probably had no idea of the depth of my interest?

I couldn't.

I did and said a lot of things during these months that I am not proud of, but this one is near the top of the list. Not even the knowledge that I agonized over this choice and that it wasn't motivated by malice redeems it much. It simply underscores the fact that the way I decided to deal with this dilemma was the culmination of a series of preceding, smaller decisions made in weakness.

It was cowardly, after our early and blithe joking about marriage, *not* to be transparent with Jason when I started to have more serious doubts about whether we would have a future together. Or, more to the point since Jason had made his intentions perfectly clear, whether we *should* have a future together.

It was cowardly, when I began to feel pressured in a self-created routine of nightly phone calls not to simply say something like, "Jason, I love talking to you, but I think we've moved a bit fast to build on what is so far a shaky foundation. Could we perhaps slow it down a bit? Maybe we should start by talking every two or three days?"

It was cowardly, instead, to start to let his calls go to voice mail or his text messages stay unanswered. (For a little while, anyway. Because the internal tension engendered by not answering the phone was never eased until I had returned the call or text and subtly re-ascertained two basic facts: that he still loved me and that he wasn't angry.)

It takes two to tango, and Jason did his bit to contribute to the unhealthy communication dynamics we established. But my part was being so driven by a need to be loved by him – even when I was not at all sure that I loved *him* as he wanted – that I avoided conflict with him at any cost.

Vancouver, Canada

I TOLD EVERYONE INVOLVED (Jason and Ryan included) that I was going to Vancouver for work, braved LAX on a sunny Friday morning, and landed in the city of my birth on a cold, rainy afternoon. As I walked into the arrivals area I was suddenly desperately nervous and acutely aware that although I felt I knew Ryan's mind fairly well, I had no idea which body housed that mind. I didn't even know the color of his hair or how tall he was.

He knew what *I* looked like. Early on I'd decided that if there was zero chemistry on either side it would be better if we learned that sooner rather than later, but I'd never been able to figure out a way to subtly ask him to send me a photo. So I'd done the next best thing. I'd mass emailed my entire mailing list with several photographs of me from the past year (me in Kenya, me in San Francisco, me smiling prettily) with the sole aim of letting him check me out. He had not reciprocated, but he hadn't stopped emailing me either, which I figured meant he hadn't ruled me out.

Either that or he was markedly less calculating than I suspected he was capable of being and had no idea at all what I was up to.

"I'll find *you*," he had cockily written the day before our rendezvous when I pointed out that I'd never seen a photo of him and would have no way of locating him in the arrivals lounge.

I had to wait twelve long minutes before he approached from behind. He turned out to be tall, with curly blond hair and thoughtful blue eyes, and much more diffident than the Ryan of the written word.

We hugged a hello and almost instantly I felt a weight lift. No Technicolor fireworks had gone off – the sort that had always let me know before that I was caught hook, line, and sinker until the story played itself out – and I thought of Jason, smiled, and was relieved. The disappointment didn't come until later. I went to bed that night tired and cleanly empty, feeling freer.

I never did come right out and try to explain to Ryan why I was really up in Vancouver. I couldn't articulate it in any way that made it sound remotely sensible, even to myself. So Ryan and I wandered a wet city for the weekend and talked instead of humanitarian work, restlessness, rootlessness, and writing.

We talked of adventure and of home.

And I watched him watching me.

For the first time, I really understood what can make people nervous when they are faced with a psychologist. There are at least ten levels to Ryan and I saw only five of them, at most, that weekend. He was much more inscrutable and guarded in person than he was on paper. I knew that there were plenty of things he was thinking through that I couldn't even guess at, but one thing he couldn't corral completely were his eyes. He *watched* me, a small smile on his lips, as if he were both baffled and amused by what he saw.

Which when I thought about it seemed entirely fair. I certainly had no grounds to complain about anyone being guarded or confused.

After a weekend of watching, rain, art galleries, and long talks over Canadian beer, I was able to get back on the plane with the mystery removed and a new friendship cemented, knowing that if Ryan had been the only obstacle standing in the way of loving Jason, that obstacle was gone.

Except – and this took me three more messy months to figure out – Ryan hadn't been the only obstacle.

I had really wanted him to be. I agonized over what was wrong with me, what prevented me from loving such a fundamentally decent man who cared so much for me. But in the end, I realized that if I stayed with Jason it would be in large part because of fear. Fear of hurting someone I cared for very deeply. Fear of disappointing him and making him angry. Fear that I couldn't trust my own instincts – that I was being hasty and turning my face away from the possibility of great happiness or that I was simply incapable of the sort of commitment Jason wanted.

Fear that I would never find someone else who loved me and that I would ultimately end up alone.

But in the end, I knew that regardless of whether I was making the biggest mistake of my life in saying no to Jason, being scared of all of these things was just not a good enough reason to get married, that I would be doing us both wrong if I said yes.

Baltimore, USA

THREE YEARS LATER I looked at the last line I'd written in my latest letter to Mike: "When it came right down to it, my primary motivation for writing my first essay was to catch someone's attention. Yes, translate that to: to impress a guy."

So how much more of this tale *was* I willing to share at this stage? What else would need to be added as an addendum to put it into context?

Perhaps that it had been almost three years since Jason and I had parted ways.

That I hadn't dated anyone else since.

That I started writing the essays largely because it was fun, but I kept writing them even when it wasn't nearly as much fun because I sensed that it was an important discipline for me to cultivate – that in the face of a constant kaleidoscope of airports and faces it would serve me well to learn to narrow my focus to a moment. To take that moment for what it was and to think carefully about what else it could be.

That over time, without my even really noticing, writing had become a spiritual discipline – one way for me to snatch breaths from beneath the waterfall of life.

That now, like the chemicals on a photographic negative, it is the keyboard that helps me define my experiences. On my best days, a jumble of moments, like so many bright pixels, coalesce into something vibrant and evocative as I type. Often I feel as if I have not understood anything of what an experience has really meant to me until I have anchored it in text.

No, apart from the "key lessons learned about long-distance relationships" that I'd already provided in my first email, I wasn't ready to lay all this out before Mike. Not yet.

What to say then?

"Why do I write essays and post them online?" I wrote. "It only took one essay to discover that I really did enjoy writing them and that people on my mailing list really liked them. The essays became something that helped me feel connected to people back home and helped them feel that they knew some of what was going on in my life. For me, they also became an important writing discipline, an important living discipline."

"I must go to sleep. I'm exhausted, which I blame in part on my sister for keeping me up talking too late last night and in part on you for keeping me up emailing the night before," I finished. "I'm heading back to L.A. tomorrow. I know you're off island-hopping again soon and will have intermittent access to email. So safe travels, and when you're near a net connection and a keyboard, write me more rambly emails."

Los Angeles – Accra – Washington, D.C. – Sydney – Zagreb – South Bend – Nairobi – San Diego – Atlanta – **Madang** – Kona – Canberra – London – Baltimore – Itonga – Vancouver – Harare – Dushanbe – Lira – Petats – Port Moresby – Brisbane – Ballina – Malibu

THE INTERNAL AND UNWINNABLE WAR

Los Angeles, USA

I RETURNED TO L.A. late the next night to find a dusty bedroom and a knee-high stack of junk mail. The apartment was blessedly silent. A note on the fridge informed me that my flatmate, Travis, was in Las Vegas for three more days, and I breathed a sigh of relief. I rather desperately hoped that when he returned it would be in a different state of mind from the one he'd been in for most of the previous eight months. I dropped my luggage in the hallway and headed straight upstairs to bed, planning to sleep until forever.

The following morning, however, found me awake at six, exhausted and cursing jet lag for being such an efficient alarm clock. The dawn light was just starting to filter into my bedroom and I lay still and warm for a moment and listened to the lambent splash of the fountain outside my window. In that tiny window of peace, fragments from the previous month came to visit.

A workshop participant's story, confided in hushed and hurried tones during a coffee break, of how her husband was abusing her. Another participant's glance sideways as he relayed how his wife had been killed in a motorcycle accident just two months earlier.

As I swung my feet out of bed I began the process of easing back into my life in California. The time away receded just a little as my bare toes met carpet, and I felt guilty as I saw it go. But I hadn't yet learned the trick of keeping two worlds equally close, and California was here, now.

At 7 a.m. on a Sunday, the streets of Pasadena were almost empty, but Noah's Bagel Shop was warm and bright against the gray skies outside. I ordered coffee and a bagel, only then remembering that it would be the first thing I'd eaten in almost twenty-four hours.

I sat in the corner on a high stool and stared out the window. Past the glass, a man paged through the paper with a frown, his foot anchoring the end of the leash. Golden ears framed two brown eyes that watched eagerly for any sign of affection. The dog's gaze didn't shift in the five minutes it took me to eat the bagel, but no affection was forthcoming.

Beside me, an elegant silver-haired woman spilled the hot water for her tea across the bench. It spread in a warm river toward a young man's paper, its headlines shouting at us about casualties in Iraq, and she blushed as he jumped up to get napkins.

"I was worried about that," she confided to the room at large. "That was the worst thing I could think of that would happen to me today."

I smiled politely and told her to look on the bright side, that since the worst had already happened, her day could only get better.

As I glanced back out the window to check whether the man had petted the dog yet, it struck me as odd that there is a place in this world where someone can say without any hint of self-deprecation that that worst thing she could imagine happening to her that day was to spill the water for her tea. Instead of feeling annoyed, I felt safe.

I congratulated myself on how smoothly my readjustment to normal life was progressing as I got up and wandered into the gourmet supermarket next door, where I stood so long in front of the milk selection that a clerk approached me with gentle trepidation and asked if he could help me. I was tempted to hand him my basket and tell him to do my shopping. Instead I smiled the enigmatic smile of someone who is so preoccupied by important thoughts that she can be immobilized with no warning in the milk aisle, reached out my hand, and took the first carton I touched.

"No thanks," I said. "I'm fine."

I wasn't, though. Not completely. I'd made it only halfway through the caramel latte I'd ordered and I was starting to feel sick. I couldn't find sausages fit for pasta sauce, and I suddenly lost patience with the whole process. Dropping my coffee into the trash I headed for the checkout with just three bananas, raspberries, red chili paste, and the milk. Maybe shopping would be easier later in the day.

Outside Noah's the man turned the page of his paper and the dog inched forward, bottom vibrating, shiny black nose almost touching a knee, but the man didn't look up or reach out. On the other side of the fence that separated us, I dropped my bag of groceries to the pavement, propped my foot on the low railing and bent to fiddle with my shoe. When the dog spared me a glance, I wiggled my fingers at him, a covert offer. Tail moving in acknowledgement, he licked my hand in one furtive, warm swipe. Then his gaze returned to the back of the paper. It was clearly not my attention that he wanted.

I wiped my hand on my jeans, picked up the bag, and headed for the car.

Sometimes arriving home from a work trip will fill me with a sudden, sweet burst of energy and the sense of a fresh page turning. I've learned to ride this energy as far as it will take me when it come – the gym, the grocery store, the washing machine. That flat fatigue that follows extended travel is often tempered if the house is clean, my suitcases are unpacked and I have something to eat when it hits.

This time there was no sweet surge of energy. The apartment felt empty and foreign. I couldn't even summon the strength to hoist my heavy suitcases up the stairs, and with Travis gone there was no one else to care if they stayed in the living room, spilling their contents across the carpet. I sighed every time I thought about packing for my next flight to Vancouver in a week. I ate bananas, soup, and toasted pita bread for two days before I could be bothered to brave the grocery store again. It was all I could do to get up, go to the office, and keep track of the radio interviews about my novel that I'd told my publisher I'd do when I returned.

Actually, I didn't always do that, either. Two mornings after getting back, the phone rang just as I was getting out of the shower. I grabbed a towel and ran to fetch it. By the time I picked it up I was at least awake enough not to tell Luke Zuckerman from some station in Ohio that (1) I had totally forgotten we were scheduled to talk live on air and (2) I wasn't wearing any clothes.

I WAS FEELING MORE at home in the apartment and in my own skin by the time Travis got back from Las Vegas, which was good because I needed that extra energy to focus on him.

When he first moved in, Travis had been the most entertaining of housemates to share the apartment with, part stand-up comic and part debate partner. By the time we'd been living together for almost two years, we had settled into a relationship that was vaguely reminiscent of siblings.

We shared the shopping and kept a running tally of money owed on the refrigerator door. We cooked for each other. We sat in the living room together sometimes on Saturdays, me writing and him working on the latest short-film project he hoped would be his ticket to making it big in Hollywood. We had a lot of mock arguments and occasionally some real ones. He got cranky at me for not doing enough of the cleaning. I got cranky at him for turning the TV up too loud late at night. Way more often than not, however, our exchanges ended in laughter. Then, slowly, subtly, things started to shift.

Even now, armed with hindsight, it's hard to know when it started.

Travis had always carried a certain energy with him, an intensity. I can't put my finger on exactly when and how that intensity stopped being just healthy fuel for his creativity and started herding his mind toward darker places, but about eight months earlier, right around my thirty-first birthday, we had started laughing less.

Around this time, Travis was deep in the throes of finishing the editing of his second short film, a disturbing tale of choice and consequences. Because he was an audiovisual consultant for large corporate shows, his work schedule had always been erratic, but now he stopped working altogether to focus on wrapping the project and start writing the script for what he hoped would be his first feature film. He sat in front of his computer until all hours of the night, going over that short film frame by frame. He covered the south wall of his bedroom entirely with flip-chart paper, marked a giant story arc on it, and started sketching out the plot he had in mind.

After being up until four or five every night, he'd often sleep until midday and then be flat and distracted in the evenings. As the summer wore on, he slowly became more and more tightly wound and less and less fun to live with. It seemed that all the genuine cheerfulness was being leached out of his intensity and replaced with a simmering hostility.

He started to take everything more personally. He bantered less and ranted more. His colleagues, other friends, the world in general – they all became the subject of extended vitriolic diatribes over the kitchen bench while one of us cooked dinner. One night he yelled at me over an innocent flippant remark. It was an attack that left me stunned, hurt, and confused.

For the first time, I started to think seriously about moving out, something I was loath to do. I'd lived in that apartment longer than I'd lived in any other place, and the second half of the year was booked solid with international travel and the book release. Where would I find the time and energy to move?

I thought it would pass. I mean, what artist *hasn't* had periods of deep immersion in serious projects when life looked grim and he felt decidedly unbalanced? Travis had wanted to be a director since he was a little boy. Films were his life passion. But right on the cusp of turning thirty, living in a city where so many glossy teenagers walk red carpets, he was feeling an incredible amount of self-induced pressure.

Then in August of that year, while I was away in Turkey for

a month, Travis lost his internal footing.

———⟨∞∞⟩———

HE WAS STARRING IN a reality TV show, Travis explained
to me less than ten minutes after I walked through the door the
night that I returned from Turkey. He had been starring in this
show ever since he was a little boy, since he first decided that he
wanted to be a director, since it first became apparent that he was
autistic.

"But you're *not* autistic," I said that night, too stunned at first
to be anything but confused by what he was saying.

"I *am*," he insisted, flicking a lock of red hair off his
forehead with a nervous sweep of a wrist. Always lean, he
was thinner than he had been when I left, and pale, with dark
shadows under his eyes. "I've done all this research online. All
the symptoms fit."

"Travis, I worked with autistic kids for six months after
graduating from high school," I said. "You're *not* autistic."

"I have Asperger's," he said.

"No you don't," I said. "You are perfectly capable of
empathy and reading social cues related to sarcasm and irony.
You choose to *ignore* social cues sometimes, but you can read
them."

"I knew you'd say that," he said. "You're all saying
something like that. But I know the truth now."

"The truth about the TV show?" I asked hesitantly.

"*Duh*," he looked at me as if he'd expected more. "Kid with
autism grows up wanting to become a director and makes it big
in Hollywood. *Great* story for reality TV! Don't tell me you
don't know what I'm talking about. I *know* you do."

"I don't," I said and then tried a different tack. "Tell me how
you figured it out."

"They made a mistake," he said, triumphant. "I already suspected, you know. But then I went out for dinner *weeks* ago with D.J. and there were lights and a camera crew outside. When we walked past they followed us. And, inside, there was a famous director sitting at a table nearby. D.J. denied the whole thing, but I totally figured it out."

"This is L.A.," I reminded him – he who'd worked as an extra on more movies than I could count. "There are camera crews everywhere."

"*Exactly*," he said.

Dead end.

"You said you already suspected by that point," I said. "When did you *first* start to suspect?"

"Right after you left I went to a bachelor party," he said. "They put something in my drink. I'm telling you, it really messed with my head."

"What was it?" I asked.

Again that look in his eyes, that look of mingled suspicion and pity at my stupidity.

"I don't *know,*" he said. "I didn't see them put it in there. I wouldn't have drunk it if I did, would I?"

"Did you take anything else?"

"No," he said. "Only pot."

"Only *pot*?"

"Only pot, no cocaine or anything else this time, I swear," he said, misunderstanding my question.

"Maybe the pot—"

"I always do pot," he said. "I do it here all the time."

He did? How had I never smelled it in the house or realized he was high? How dumb *was* I?

"Pot can make you paranoid," I said, using that word out loud for the first time.

"No," he said. "Pot takes the edge off. It doesn't flip me out like whatever that poison was that they gave me at the party."

Dead end.

"So, when you say, 'They're all in on it', who are *they*?" I asked.

"Everyone," he said. He looked suddenly and acutely miserable.

"My parents must have been in on it right from the beginning," he said. "I don't blame them. Really, I don't, because they knew I wanted to be a director and they thought this would only help. But why didn't they see the pressure that would come when I found out? Didn't they know that I wouldn't be able to trust anything? That I would wonder if every friendship in my life was a lie?"

"So all your friends are in on it?"

"Yeah, how could they not be? The networks would need their cooperation."

"Me?"

"Yes," he said and then wavered. "I think so. I'm not sure. I don't know."

"I'm not," I said.

"I *want* to believe you," he said. "But everyone's just saying the same thing – that they're not part of it. That it's not happening. And I *know* it is. I just need someone to level with me. That's all I'm asking, that *someone* tell me the truth."

Dead end.

"Is there anyone you trust right now?" I asked.

"The girl at the video store," he said. "She smiled at me yesterday. I think she'd tell me the truth."

"Have you ever talked to her?"

"No."

Dead end.

Dead end.

Dead end.

"I've *got* to go to bed," I finally said that night in August. "I have to go to work tomorrow."

"Fine," Travis said, looking frustrated and drawn under the bright glare of the kitchen lights. His hair was tousled; he clearly hadn't combed it that day.

He leaned across the bench toward me, beckoned conspiratorially, and whispered.

"I think you know exactly what I'm talking about. But just in case you don't, you should know ... *they're watching us from behind the mirrors.*"

AFTER SEVERAL DAYS OF talking almost nonstop about this reality TV show while I scrambled to figure out what might be wrong with him, Travis went quiet on the subject. By the time I left for Kenya and Ghana, things seemed almost back to normal. Travis was still jittery and edgy but not, I thought, psychotic. I began to wonder whether the whole episode may have been drug-induced and temporary, but it was the final push I needed to make up my mind once and for all that I was definitely moving out within six months – the soonest my schedule seemed to permit.

Now, after a month apart while I was in Africa, I nervously awaited his return from Las Vegas. Would he be the Travis that I had moved in with – quick-witted, sarcastic, and thoughtful – or would he be suspicious and unreachable?

When he walked through the door I was relieved to see that he seemed fine at first glance. He was friendly, upbeat, and interested in how my time away had been.

"Are you still emailing that guy in Papua New Guinea?" he

asked after I'd filled him in on a few highlights.

"Why is it," I asked, "that I come back from Africa and all anyone wants to do is talk about this?"

"What do you mean *anyone?*" Travis asked. "How many people have you told this story to, anyway? And we want to talk about it because it's *weird.*"

"I haven't told many people, actually," I said. "And it's not that weird."

"Are you still emailing?" Travis asked.

"Yes," I said. "When he has internet, anyway."

"So, what, you're, like, dating now?"

"No," I said. "We're just getting to know each other."

Travis looked at me in a way that let me know he didn't buy a word of it.

"What are you writing about in all those letters?"

"Our childhoods," I said. "Our families, our work, what our day has been like, or whatever it is that we're thinking about at the time. I don't know, we never seem to run out of things to write about."

"You're not dating," Travis said, "but you're writing this guy letters how often, every day?"

"No," I said, my tone edging toward that frequently used on annoying younger siblings. "Just three or four times a week. Maybe five."

"You're crazy," Travis said cheerfully. "What are you going to do, just keep emailing each other like this for the next ten years?"

"I have no idea," I said, shrugging and suddenly unbothered by this line of teasing. It was so hard to explain the sense of peace I had about the whole situation. I always got a little thrill to see a letter from Mike in my inbox, but on days when there wasn't one I didn't obsess about it either. I didn't feel any pressure or sense of urgency. And I deliberately hadn't let myself think too far down the track or forecast some sort of ending to our current correspondence.

"What are you doing tonight?" I asked Travis, changing the subject.

He glanced at his watch, jumped up, and headed for the stairs.

"I have a date," he said over his shoulder. "A normal one, not the writing-letters kind."

"We are *not* dating," I called after him.

"Whatever," he said.

Mike, Papua New Guinea

MIKE'S NEXT LETTER ARRIVED the next day.

"Right now there is a tremendous tropical downpour," it began. "You know, the sort when you can taste the moisture in the air as you hear the rain pounding on the roof. When I experience those types of rain it brings back memories of sitting on the front porch in Uganda after a hard sweaty day's work, listening to jazz on my iPod, feeling the winds sweep in much-needed refreshment. The bad side of these types of rains is that they make everything you own turn moldy. But who needs clothes and leather shoes when you have memories like that?

"Now, after rereading the end of your last letter, let me pause for a second and allow me to point out that blaming your own shortcomings on others is perhaps not the most healthy of coping strategies to get you through life. I take no blame in your inability to manage to get to bed at a sensible hour. But in the spirit of camaraderie among fellow travelers on the journey, allow me to pass on to you a most excellent coping strategy I learned during my time in Tajikistan. Here it is: blame all your problems on (drumroll) Uzbekistan!

"That's right. All problems, any problems, any time, it's Uzbekistan's fault. The Tajiks are legendary at it. Price of flour rising in the market? Uzbekistan is blocking trucks. No gas in the mains? Uzbekistan is blocking the pipeline. Overcast, gloomy day? All that dust stirred up in Uzbekistan is blowing over. It seemed odd at first, but I've come to embrace this strategy. Whenever I have one of those crap moments at work, 'Damn Uzbekistan!' Or when I feel particularly lonely or isolated or frustrated 'It's all Uzbekistan's fault!' and I instantly feel better. So next time you're in need of a scapegoat for any problem you may face, don't forget that the lovely land of the Uzbeks is at your disposal.

"And, yes, the internal and unwinnable war between the longing for adventure and home. You described it well in your last letter. Last year before I left Melbourne I went on a little personal retreat at an Ignatian Spirituality Centre. One of the things that came out of that time was a 'mapping' of those desires as different branches of the same tree.

"I want challenge, adventure, intensity, purpose.

"And I want stable friendships, reasonable comfort, security.

"At the time it seemed like it was all well and good for those different branches to stem from the trunk of 'I want to love and to be loved' and it still does. But on a weekly basis those branches duke it out a bit for prominence as far as which one holds more roosting birds at night. Not sure which branch produces more fruit, though."

Lisa, USA

"THE INTERNAL AND UNWINNABLE war. Hmmm, how many birds roost in your branches at night, generally? Which type of bird is your favorite? Which branches are their favorites? What type of tree are you? I think I would like to be a jacaranda tree."

Mike, Papua New Guinea

"TREES. I'D LIKE TO be a poinciana tree with those beautiful orange blossoms screaming out from the forest canopy with passion and vigor. And I'd like to be the white oak tree spreading its magnificent sturdy branches into the air, and a eucalyptus tree defying drought, and a douglas fir because their green is so deep and rich that the candles just don't do it any justice, and a ponderosa pine whose needles give off the most delightful odor when they hit the ground in the warm air of summer, and a banyan tree with its impressive roots that seem to grow up out of the ground, and the mango tree in Uganda at the center of the displaced peoples camp where everyone gathers for meetings. So you want to know how many birds roost, and what types of birds, and where they like to roost, and which branches need pruning, and I can't even decide what type of tree I want to be.

"When is your next trip – to Vancouver, right? What are you doing up there? Is Ryan Schmidt in Vancouver these days?"

Lisa, USA

"I GO UP TO Vancouver on Friday to do an interview for a TV station. It's a show called *The Standard* that interviews people about how their faith influences their work as a public figure. It's partly book publicity, but we'll mostly be talking faith and work – neither of which topics I'm super excited to be discussing on national television, come to think of it.

"Apparently the station is sending a car to pick me up from the airport. They'll do my hair and makeup and that's all I know. Television. Freaky. No doubt it will make for a good essay, though. Well, probably a better essay if I manage to get into a coughing fit or fall off the back of the couch or something like that, but I sort of hope that doesn't happen on live television."

Mike, Papua New Guinea

"INTERVIEW IN VANCOUVER SOUNDS cool. How faith influences people's work. Yep, definitely a worthwhile topic. Don't go out of your way to fall off the back of a couch. I just think it's so uncool when people sabotage their TV appearances so that they can write up a cool essay about it later.

"Do you ask for a window or an aisle seat on planes (or the middle)? Are you one of those ultra-purpose-driven acid-tripping zealots who specifically ask for the middle seat so that they have not one but two people upon whom they can inflict their beliefs?! Don't laugh too hard, in a former life I used to ask for the middle seat from time to time."

Lisa, USA

"UM, I THINK YOU might be a better Christian than I am. Not only have I never requested the middle seat for the purposes of inflicting my views upon my fellow travelers, the idea has never even entered my head before (and lots of ideas have entered my head – most of them positively *wicked* in comparison with this idea). What's worse, if the good Lord himself informed me in no uncertain terms that he specifically wanted me to request a middle seat from here to Vancouver, I would probably do it.

But I doubt I'd manage to muster up any semblance of good grace about it until later, when I was writing about the whole incident with a wry sort of humor that can substitute quite well for actually *having* that good grace. Sort of like aspartame almost tastes like sugar. Almost, but you can taste the hollow underneath if you pay attention.

"I do not particularly like the person I become when I step into airports. Increasingly I am catching myself feeling resentful, and entitled, and scornful, and impatient. I endure. I daydream about desert islands. I sometimes send out 'don't even think about talking to me' vibes. And if for some freak reason I get stuck in the middle, I suffer."

Mike, Papua New Guinea

"LIST OF THINGS THAT Mike hasn't done in the last decade: change email addresses, purchase a new vehicle, and ask for a middle seat.

"Faith/belief is a toughie for me. I definitely don't think I'm a better Christian. Or that the word 'better' should even be mentioned in the context of faith (unless of course it's laced with sarcasm, then it's entirely appropriate). And I truly doubt that your faith is 100% like aspartame, although if you ever have feelings along those lines I wouldn't be surprised.

"So how do you react when you feel that parts of your life are becoming more aspartame than sugar? What do you do?

"I struggle. But deep down I want to be genuine.

"And I reckon you do, too.

"Looking back now (with all the wisdom of a 31-year-old who's acquired some bruises in the school of hard knocks in life and faith) I see that I used to view the world as black and white. Subconsciously and quite arrogantly, I believed that faith and life were like a series of formulas and 'best practices' and that if you followed the formulas and best practices, then everything would work out okay for you.

"Fuck. Fuuuuck.

"If only it were like that.

"Part of me has (truly) come to celebrate that life and faith aren't confined to formulas. Part of me celebrates the mystery and magic of life.

"And part of me says, 'Damn, it's frustrating' and deep down wishes that the world would just behave the way I thought it did back when I was in my 20s and I had it all figured out.

"So what do you think about faith? How have your ideas about faith changed over the past 10ish years? How have your ideas about faith expanded and contracted as you've come face-to-faith with tragedies of human existence and as you've encountered people from different cultures and worldviews and faith walks?

"And how do you keep that historical baggage stuff from depressing you about faith? I struggle. I think as I get older (and perhaps a bit softer, or perhaps a bit less edgy in my anger about injustice, or perhaps a bit more graceful???) I find myself reacting less strongly than I used to. I still feel ashamed and angry and confused about how people who were sincerely trying to adhere to the same faith to which I'm trying to adhere could have enslaved Africans and shipped them off to deepest darkest America, for instance. But then, perhaps future generations will come to places like Vanuatu and Ghana and Afghanistan and judge us harshly for our neocolonialism in all our good-natured aid and development work.

"So my last point, because I need to get out of the office as they're closing in two minutes. And it's a question, one that I trust you'll answer truthfully and straightforwardly. So what do you think of me trying to come down to Australia sometime between Jan 10 and Feb 6 while you're there? I'd like to try. If you think that would be okay."

Los Angeles – Accra – Washington, D.C. – **Sydney** – Zagreb – **South Bend** – Nairobi – San Diego – Atlanta – Madang – Kona – Canberra – London – Baltimore – Itonga – **Vancouver** – **Harare** – Dushanbe – Lira – Petats – Port Moresby – Brisbane – Ballina – Malibu

THE VALLEY OF THE SHADOW OF THE GOLDEN DOME

33,000 feet

A WEEK LATER I was on the plane to Vancouver and lucky to be there. I hadn't banked on the pouring rain that greeted me when I got up at 3:30 a.m. to head to the airport for my six o'clock flight. That was an understandable miscalculation – a deluge like that in L.A. is a once-a-year event, if that. What was not so understandable was forgetting that the city of Vancouver lived in an entirely separate country. When I rushed into the airport at 5:13, damp and frazzled and handed my passport to the woman behind the desk she was not at all impressed.

"This is an international flight," she said sharply. "Another two minutes and the system wouldn't have let me check you in even if I wanted to."

"Oh, yeah," I said lamely. "Sorry. I forgot."

This earned me a look of complete scorn, but she checked me in.

In addition to forgetting that Canada was a sovereign nation, I'd also forgotten to pack a book. So takeoff found me with nothing to do but stare at the back of the seat in front of me and think about the interview I'd give that afternoon and about Mike and his questions.

Not the question he'd asked about whether I'd like him to come to Australia in six weeks – that one had been easy to answer. I had emailed him back immediately, carefully light.

"I think that would be a lot of fun if it worked out," I had said.

No, it was the other questions he'd asked that I was still stuck on.

"What do you think about faith? How have your ideas about faith changed over the past decade as you've come face-to-faith with tragedies of human existence and as you've encountered people from different worldviews and faith walks?"

"How do you keep that historical baggage stuff from depressing you about faith?"

"What do you do when you feel parts of your faith are becoming more aspartame than sugar?"

How could I travel around the world running workshops on the intersection of humanitarian work and spirituality – how could I be flying up to sit for an interview on national television about this stuff – and still not have a clear answer to these questions?

―――― ⊕⊗⊖ ――――

IN MY FIRST NOVEL, I wrote about the spiritual struggles of

a narrator named Cori – a teen who finds herself caught up in a civil war in Indonesia:

> *Church probably came first – that's as far back*
> *as I can remember. Whether we were in Australia or*
> *Kenya, Sunday morning found the five of us in church*
> *and afterward in an ice cream shop. Given that African*
> *church services regularly go for more than two hours,*
> *Tanya, Luke and I earned every bite.*
>
> *Sweet bribery aside, God was a constant centering*
> *force in a kaleidoscope of airports, cultures, and friends.*
> *I was baptized at our church in Nairobi when I was*
> *fourteen. In the middle of winter. In an unheated*
> *baptismal pool. Outdoors.*
>
> *That's how important God was to me.*
>
> *I guess I wasn't quite holy enough not to feel the*
> *cold that day. But I also felt something else: a deep*
> *surety, as warm as touch, that my life was an important*
> *piece in the huge cosmic puzzle. That God loved me.*
> *That I had purpose.*
>
> *Even before this summer, that was what I felt*
> *slipping away.*

I was baptized at sixteen in Zimbabwe, but those two minor details aside, this part of Cori's story is all mine. I donated it to her and cloaked it in fiction, but I can claim it as truth right down to the cold water, the two siblings, and the post-church ice cream.

Actually, in terms of home anchored in place, church probably outranks even airports. Church is there as far back as I can remember.

In Bangladesh we went to church in a simple cement building, with poverty crouched just outside the door. I can dredge up glimpses of fans slowly stirring the heavy heat, worn hymnals with cracked spines, a clinky and out-of-tune piano, and the Australian missionaries making jokes at the New Zealanders' expense.

It all stood in rather stark contrast with our next church home in the United States, with its hyper-adrenalinated children's program stocked with summer camps, ski trips, Thanksgiving skits involving stuffed toy turkeys and real chain saws, and much talk of the rapture.

For those of you who didn't grow up going to church in the United States during the 1980s, *the rapture* is the phrase generally used to refer the moment when Jesus will return to earth, pick up all the Christians, and take them off to hang out in heaven.

Many theories abounded about when the rapture would occur and what, exactly, would happen. Most of my Sunday-school teachers seemed to believe that all the Christians would be suddenly whisked up to heaven sometime during seven years of suffering and tribulation that was destined to befall the earth during the "end times". And in the face of a bleak economic forecast and the specter of the Soviet Union as the great evil of the modern world, many also believed that the end times were upon us *right then*.

The rapture would probably occur within the next five years or so, these people generally posited, and on that wonderful day Jesus would float down from the clouds to the great and glorious sound of angelic trumpets and all the true Christians would rise up to greet him in a midair reunion.

There were other theories about the rapture. Lots of other theories.

I think the main point of all this rapture talk was to impel us to convince all our friends of their need to be saved before the imminent arrival of the big day with its attendant and eternal separation of the sheep and the goats. But I didn't have many friends to preach to at eleven. I just had plenty of time to research the rapture the way I researched most other things in life, by reading novels.

Long before the popular *Left Behind* series, there were a slew of other stories about the end times, most of which I ferreted out and devoured. In retrospect, I doubt that this was entirely healthy fuel for an already-feverish imagination. I spent far too much time wondering what would happen to me if the rapture occurred while I was changing clothes or, horrors, sitting on the toilet. Would I be sucked into the sky *naked*? On at least one occasion I got out of the shower to the sound of silence, a palpable atmospheric emptiness that triggered a sudden and visceral certainty that I was completely alone in the house and probably in the world. Had everyone I knew and loved gone off to meet Jesus without me?

When Mum and Dad sat us down one day when I was twelve and asked us what we thought of moving to Africa, I figured that if Jesus were coming back within the next five years anyway, Africa was as good a place as any to go and have an adventure in the meantime.

Which took me to church in Zimbabwe.

Harare, Zimbabwe

CHURCH IN ZIMBABWE WAS long. Looooong. During the first couple of years we were there, I had limited patience for the sermons that often went for an hour without any chain saw-based entertainment at all. Mum played music for the service and Dad taught one of the adult Sunday school classes. That meant that we were at church on Sundays from eight in the morning until almost one in the afternoon.

Looooong.

By sixteen, however, I wasn't going to church just on Sunday mornings. I was also heading back there voluntarily on Sunday nights for the evening service.

Part of me would like to be able to claim that this newfound interest in all things church was solely the result of an inner awakening to the sacred, a deep personal spiritual fervor.

It wasn't.

Not unless a budding teenage awareness of the divine mystery posed by the opposite sex counts as spiritual fervor.

Yes. Boys. The youth group went out for coffee after the evening service. This was a big deal. I went to an all-girls school, and opportunities for hanging out with boys were limited. Church was the center of my social life, and the friends I made there, the first real friends I'd ever had, introduced me to all sorts of things, including how to drive a car, ride a motorcycle, and drink vodka.

But my friends in Zimbabwe served as guides for much more than the odd and relatively tame foray into the adventures of vodka and lemonade. They also taught me how to dance and to laugh, and just as the concept of friendship came alive for me during that time, so did the concept of God. However mixed my motivations for embracing church, I eventually found more than boys there.

The pastor at our church in Harare was a man named Peter Griffith. A decade before I walked into his church, Peter had been living with his family and thirteen others at Elim Mission in the north of the country. In 1978, during the civil war that transformed Rhodesia into Zimbabwe, guerrillas armed with machetes crossed the border with Mozambique, entered the mission compound, and murdered everyone there: nine adults and four children, including a three-week-old baby. Peter and his family survived only because they were in England at the time.

The Griffith family returned to Africa, where Peter accepted a senior position in the education department of the newly formed Zimbabwean government. In a society collectively wounded by years of fighting – trying to find a way out of the devastation and plagued by ongoing controversy about how to see justice done – Peter consistently maintained that forgiveness was the right path to healing.

Shortly after becoming senior pastor of a church in Harare, this public mantra was put to the test. A decade after the massacre, the youngest member of the party that had attacked Elim Mission sought Peter out and confessed his role in the killings. He'd been fourteen at the time, a youth fighting under the name "War Devil," and he'd risen to become the youngest platoon leader of the insurgency. Shortly after the war, this young man said, he'd seen a vision of the hand of God coming in judgment against him. It must have been some vision – he'd become a Christian on the spot, left the militia, and enrolled in Bible College.

In addition to his forgiveness, Peter offered this man a job as the guard and groundskeeper for our church.

This story didn't seem so extraordinary to me the first time I heard it. The war had been over for only eight years. The scars and the stories were numerous and still fresh – more than one of my friends had lost their fathers in the fighting. But over time that story started to sink in. It came to symbolize some of the strength and optimism that marked the Zimbabwe I knew and loved during the four years we lived there. Against the dark backdrop of injustice and violence, with storm clouds of coming hardship still distant on the horizon, it lit up the present with hope.

I could not have put it like this then. Then, I was only

starting to discern what faith meant to me. Then, the question for me wasn't whether God existed. As a teen, the existence of God was as self-evident to me as the need to breathe to live; my struggles with this foundation would come later. Instead, what was at stake was more the basic orientation and flavor of my faith.

Did I, could I, and would I believe in a God who loves us and intends good and right despite what I knew of all the wrongs – from meanness to murder – that people are capable of?

It was in Zimbabwe that I really answered yes to that question for the first time.

That yes wasn't a sudden and inexplicable inner flood of divinely inspired certainty. It was a cumulative yes, born from the intersection of multiple tributaries feeding into my life. It came from discovering the sweetness and security of friendship love for the first time. From thousands of small positive triumphs by others – smiles, joy, kindness – in defiance of pain or need. From slowly, so slowly, waking up to right and wrong. From the stories I read in the Bible and lived by those like Peter Griffiths. Stories that called me toward higher ground.

I was baptized at sixteen, just months before we left. I had known from the first that we would be staying in Zimbabwe for only four years. What I hadn't expected was that by the time we had to leave I would feel that I *belonged* in Africa. In the months leading up to that final farewell I begged my parents to leave me behind in Harare.

I could live with my best friend, Angie, for the next two years, I argued, and finish high school with my friends. I would come to visit my family twice a year. Clearly it was a sensible plan.

Angie's parents, I do believe, would have gone for it. Mine didn't. Even then the writing was on the wall for Zimbabwe. The last year we were there, there was a drought. Food was scarcer on the shelves, and butter, meat, and even toilet paper were rationed in stores. At times we had electricity for only five or six hours a day, and on those evenings I studied by candlelight. Inflation and the HIV infection rate in the country had started an upward spiral.

I didn't care – a luxury, I know, I could indulge only because I was a child of relative privilege and the personal impact of all of this was minimal. I always had plenty to eat and clothes to wear. I had friends I loved. I was excelling at school. For the first time in my life, I didn't feel like an outsider. As far as I was concerned, I had adopted Zimbabwe as home.

As far as my parents were concerned, it would be much wiser for me to come back to the states for the last year and a half of high school and then move to Australia, my *real* home, to attend university.

When we left Harare I carried with me many unshed tears, a wristwatch that would remain stubbornly set on Zimbabwean time for the next year and a half, and my faith, the seeds of which had only really started to flower under a fierce African sun.

Sydney, Australia

HOW EXACTLY DID THIS faith, awakened primarily by stories of grace, become quite so rigid and rule-bound during the next chapter of my life?

My sister's dodgy counselor would probably suggest that I had been abused and was seeking to exert some control over an uncertain world. A decent counselor might wonder whether being uprooted from the first place I'd ever loved as home caused me to cling more tightly to spiritual anchors that promised solace and permanence. A developmental psychologist with an interest in religion would shrug and say a legalistic brand of belief is a perfectly normal stage of spiritual development.

Whatever the reason, I became that person you want to hire as a baby-sitter for your kids. I brought my Bible with me and read it after the kids were in bed instead of watching cable TV. The summer after I graduated from high school I went on a ten-week mission trip to a remote island in the Philippines. I memorized the entire book of Philippians, then the book of James, then Ephesians. Throughout university I went to church on Sunday nights and did most of the other things that my Anglican dormitory insisted *should* be done by good Christians. I went to Bible study and evangelism training. I met weekly with my Bible-study leader or (after I became a leader) with those in my group. I went to lunchtime lectures on campus. I practically earned another degree in biblical studies.

Though I did all this, a lot of it never felt as if it fit me quite right.

In evangelism training I repeatedly ducked the assignment to approach people sitting around during lunch and ask them whether, if they died the next day, they could be *sure* they were going to heaven. I found myself in a real bind over this. I *did* believe that Jesus was the truth, the life, and the way to freedom, yet I could never quite reconcile that with my certainty that it was rude and annoying to interrupt people enjoying a peaceful lunch and accost them with questions about their eternal destiny.

"It is more important for people to think about these questions than have a peaceful lunch," my Bible-study leader insisted.

"But when people do it to me, all I want to do is tell them to piss off," I said. "I really don't think it's the best way to get the message across."

I was as comfortable in a bar or on the dance floor as I was in church, sometimes more so. I held my own Bible-study groups on the beach and occasionally we *never even opened the Bible*. I complained that my church in Sydney was high on head knowledge and low on joy. More than once certain Bible-study leaders accused me of having a bad attitude and of not respecting them.

They were largely right. But it was hard to be entirely penitent when it was the same leader who had answered a "what role should women play in church leadership?" question by advising us that women were not permitted to teach men.

"This means," he said, "that if a man has a question in Bible study and a woman knows the answer, she shouldn't say anything, because that would be teaching."

I'm leaving out all the good stuff, of course. Most of the people in church leadership would not have given this answer. Many cared deeply for others and wrestled bravely with tough questions. Some of the friends I made during this time remain among my most treasured today.

So I do not count the hours I spent in church wasted, but I can still blush when I remember how rigid and simplistic my faith was. For even as a pseudo-rebel within that conservative system, I had internalized a formula of faith that went something like this:

1. Believe ye first all the right things.
2. Don't do the wrong things (date non-Christians, have sex before marriage, drink too much, etc.).
3. Then, I believed, the kingdom of God would be added unto you and *life would make sense*.

In the end it was probably these last four words that I had attached to my tripartite salvation equation that eventually caused me to question everything else.

South Bend, USA

I WAS TWENTY-SIX AND at Notre Dame studying international peace when the wheels really fell off the train, for it was at Notre Dame that I first fell in love.

I'd dated more than a handful of guys before this, but I'd always been skeptical of that phrase *falling in love*. Love wasn't something you fell into, I thought smugly. It was something you worked to create together bit by bit. It was a decision, not just a feeling. And it was more of a campfire than a lightning bolt.

Yes, well, that might all still be good theory and maybe even good practice, but it went right out the window the first time I saw Brian.

Brian lived across the hall from me. He was six feet tall, sandy-haired, and green-eyed. He'd worked as a conflict-resolution trainer in Bosnia, a peace analyst in Rwanda, and an Armani model in Italy. Like me, he'd been born overseas and grown up in multiple countries. Unlike me, he was an atheist. And I was drawn to him with an illogical, stubborn, single-mindedness from the moment we met – the proverbial moth to a dangerously charismatic flame.

We sparked right from the start. I saw in him a fellow third-culture kid, still struggling to work out some sense of belonging yet relishing the relational "diplomatic immunity" of his outsider status; someone driven to seek raw intensity both professionally and personally by demons he couldn't fully name.

I was a paradox to him, a kindred spirit who inexplicably believed in God. He both respected me and was infuriated by me.

"How *can* you?" he interrogated me frequently and heatedly. "How *can* you still believe that the Bible is the *truth*? The sheer arrogance of that! And how *can* you believe in a loving God after everything you've seen? After Bosnia? And Indonesia? And

Rwanda, for God's sake? How *can* you, when you are as smart as you are? It makes me seriously doubt your intellect in every other domain."

"That's a bit rich, coming from someone who's been taking editing advice from me all year," I'd shoot back, trying not to let him see how his words had wounded and rattled me anew.

Other people had questioned my faith, of course, but never someone who seemed to have a personal and vested interest in dismantling my beliefs bit by bit. Never someone who made me so angry that I lost my temper and screamed at him, and swore. Never someone I provoked to such fury that he threw things and slammed doors. Never someone who made me want, more than I'd ever wanted anything else, to drag him to the nearest altar or the nearest bed – it didn't really matter much which.

For the first time in my life, I couldn't will my emotions to fall in line with my beliefs, and prayer to a god who seemed utterly silent changed my desires not one single bit. I continued to love and want Brian all year despite knowing that any marriage would almost certainly end in disaster and despite a parade of short-term interests in his life.

It was me he always came back to, me he talked to.

"They have his body for a while," I reasoned. "I always have his unguarded honesty."

It was enough. It had to be.

Much more than fighting Brian that year, I fought myself – an internal war waged against feelings I "fell" into and felt helpless to resist. I battled to make sense of it all, and to keep my distance.

I mostly lost.

It was simultaneously an exhilarating and excruciating year, and by the end of it I felt dismantled from the inside out. During this year that I attended one of the most celebrated bastions of

Catholicism in the country and lived within sight of the golden dome that crowned the basilica, my surety in the existence of God as a foundational force granting shape, meaning, and color to life dissolved.

By the time I left Notre Dame and headed for Los Angeles I wondered whether everything that I'd been taught to believe and that I'd thought I understood held even the echo of truth. Whether all those Sunday-school rules were just acting as mental and emotional blinkers that I had, in large part, dutifully accepted. Whether there was value in abstinence of any sort in life. And, of course, one that had troubled me for a good sight longer than just that year: how a loving, good, omnipotent God could possibly stand to hold back and watch the bad unfurl alongside the good in the wilderness of freedom and choice.

33,000 feet

MORE THAN FOUR YEARS later, on a flight to Vancouver, the seat-belt sign dinged off. I stood up to retrieve my laptop from the overhead bin and opened up a Word document.

How to explain all of this to Mike?

"I've told you that I came close to walking away from faith altogether," I started. "Perhaps a truer way of putting it would be that I came close to dying in my tracks faith-wise. What I came up against while working in prison didn't do it, and neither did the suffering I saw around the world. The tipping point for me came when I went to Notre Dame and fell in love with a playboy of an atheist who hated the fact that I was a Christian.

"I spun out emotionally and spiritually that year.

"I didn't do any of those things (pray, read the Bible, go to church) that I'd been bought up to believe were, if not the things that got me to heaven, at least the hallmarks of a healthy, vibrant faith. More than anything, I wanted to take a long sabbatical from being a 'good Christian' and do whatever the hell I wanted with my body and my life and my decisions about right and wrong.

"You know that foggy gray that descends sometimes? That stuck around in the core part of me for a very long time.

"But even when I was just keeping the rules for the sake of it, even when all the genuine feeling had gone out of it and I was most agonized in my doubts, I wanted there to be a god out there who loves us. I didn't want to walk away, but I did feel like I was deeply mired in some sort of enduring spiritual depression that probably accomplished much the same ends as walking away defiantly would have."

I stopped typing and stared out of the window beside me at the view, thinking of this time in my life and other questions Mike had asked me.

What had I done when my faith turned to aspartame?

I had moved to L.A. and almost crumbled under the solitary weight of loneliness during my first four months there.

I had started to drink. I was no stranger to alcohol – in Australia, drinking is right up there with mocking on the unofficial "national sports" list. But during this time I crossed a line that I had never crossed before. I started drinking alone, and then I started doing that most nights. Sometimes I drank myself to sleep on the couch, waking up to terrible headaches and empty bottles.

I had put up profiles on dating websites, looking to finally leave behind the pain of an unrequited and impossible love.

I had reveled in the nourishing warmth of Jason's affection when it was lavished on me. I let him hold me too tightly, too close, because I got something out of it, too.

I had seen the salvation of understanding in the words of

a stranger in Afghanistan and then chased him down across borders.

I had hardly stood still for a single second.

Out the window of the plane, the early-morning sun was gilding the clouds below with a fresh golden pink. It was doubtless cloudy on the ground, and still raining, but it was celestial up at thirty-three thousand feet.

The seat-belt sign came back on and a voice above my head warned me that we were about to start our descent. It was time to shut down all electronics.

I looked down at my letter to Mike and added one more line before turning off the computer.

"I don't feel like that way (spiritually depressed) anymore – most of the time, anyway."

Los Angeles, USA

SOME PIVOTS ARE SUDDEN, born of formative instants. Others are long, slow arcs. With these, the change in direction becomes clear only when you check your rearview mirror or raise your eyes to see a different vista stretching out in front of you.

This is the sort of gradual pivot that has unfolded in my life since the end of my relationship with Jason. I look back at that time now with the same odd hybrid of recognition and puzzled wonder that ambushes me whenever I see photographs of myself in high school staring down from the walls of my parents' house. In those photos my face is unlined and softly rounded. I want to reach into those images and pinch my own cheeks.

I can't believe I ever looked that young.

I can't believe how unmoored I felt during my first year and a half in California.

And now, more than three years on, I find myself in a different place.

The way I see God and the way I think God probably sees me has changed. As core issues of living faith have become less neatly edged by dos and don'ts, they have inhabited instead the far messier territory of awareness, attitude, action, and intention.

I've changed in other ways, too.

I see and feel more as it's happening, I think. The cheerful beacon of a small orange flower by the path. The grounding warmth of a cup of coffee against my palms. The triggers and trajectories of my own mood swings, and the thoughts, fears, and exhilarations they typically tow in their wake.

I value solitude more, and silence.

I'm a little less imprisoned than I was by my perceptions of what other people think of me.

But it's far easier to point to specific ways that I've become more at home in my own skin in recent years than to explain exactly how these changes came about. The catalysts weren't the same things that had galvanized me a decade earlier – or, at least, they didn't result in the same uncomplicated reaction. Services at the church of five thousand that I attended in L.A. still sometimes stirred or challenged me deeply, but they also sometimes left me cold, or contemptuous, or simply conflicted about my own judgmental attitude.

The changes that have taken place during the last couple of years certainly didn't happen during early mornings spent reading the Bible, because I wasn't doing that.

I suspect things started to shift around the time, about two years after I arrived, that I started to feel that familiar tickle pushing me to seek new pastures and I decided to stay put in Los Angeles until I had a better reason to leave than an abstract sense that my life would surely fit me more completely and more comfortably somewhere else. Anywhere else.

As odd as it might sound, staying put was the harder choice. I probably would have been more comfortable immersed in the intense dynamic of learning a new place and new people than I was meeting the challenge of continuity. But although I still longed for the adventure of change, I was also getting tired.

Increasingly I was finding myself haunted by a doubtful sort of melancholy, a constant low-level ache. On one trip to London around this time – as I wandered through the chaos of Heathrow, as I manhandled my bags up and down the Underground steps, as I ate alone in an Indian restaurant that night – I was overwhelmed with the sense that my life was fracturing so irrevocably into a thousand disconnected people, places, and sensations that I would never stand a hope of feeling fully integrated.

"The glass window facing the street is entirely patterned by a complex web of fine cracks," I wrote in my journal as I waited for my food to arrive. "It looks solid enough at first glance, but I wonder how hard I'd have to hit it to trigger a noisy shower of shiny, sharp fragments?"

To others, I knew, I looked solid enough. To others, the life I led looked fascinating, even charmed. But I was also sure that this – my habitual tendency to judge my life through the prism of others' perceptions – was itself part of the problem

"Outside of comparing, we cannot feel," Andre Acimon said when writing about the benefits of his own globetrotting. But, I was starting to wonder, when does all that change? When do all those differences, all that opportunity for comparison become too much of a good thing?

At what point does a constant stream of change *blunt* our ability to feel and connect to the present and to ourselves? At what point do we become the Transit Loungers described so poignantly by Pico Iyer as those "sitting at the Departure Gate, boarding pass in hand, watching the destinations ticking over. [Those] who feel neither the pain of separation nor the exultation of wonder; who alight with the same emotions with which we embarked; who go down to the baggage carousel and watch our lives circling, circling, circling, waiting to be claimed."

And at what point do we become such practiced chameleons – sometimes choosing to blend in, others to stand out – that we no longer know our native color?

How had I ended up with this life? And did I even want it, or was I largely enjoying playing a role others marveled at?

These questions were among the many that demanded to be addressed when, after breaking up with Jason, I slowed down long enough to hear the internal clamor, and it was mostly writing that helped me start to address them.

By the time I had been in L.A. two years, writing had elbowed its way into my life and established itself as both a core passion and a need. I had started writing my first novel without the faintest idea of why I felt compelled to do so. After it was finished I turned to journaling and essays to fill the gap it had left. Over time, without me even really noticing, writing became something I *needed* to do, and it was writing more than anything else that helped me name and face questions Pico Iyer asked me, and others that I asked myself.

How did I answer when a friend asked me whether I was "fulfilled"?

What did I think of when I heard the word *hope*?

How did I really feel about being by myself when my younger sister announced she was pregnant or yet another good friend got engaged?

What could pull me back from the edge when, temporarily overwhelmed by the scope of tragedy and pain in this world,

I felt temped to level the playing field and join others in their distress?

Usually it wasn't that I found great *answers* to these sorts of questions while writing. It was more that the writing forced me to stick a flag in the sand, no matter how small, and say *something*. It pushed me to figure out what I actually thought and wanted rather than simply reacting to a constantly revolving merry-go-round of people and events. It helped transform happenings, thoughts, and moods into things acknowledged, clarified, and manageable.

It made me commit to being more myself.

It made me own my life.

Vancouver, Canada

I'D TOLD MIKE THAT I was nervous about the interview I was flying to Canada for, and it turned out that I had good reason to be. In addition to the expected discussion of work and my novel, the host of the show didn't hesitate to venture into completely unexpected and far more difficult territory.

"With all your experience and training," he asked me during the second half of the interview, "what do *you* think we should be doing in Sudan?"

"You've worked in the past with sex offenders – are these people redeemable, are they fixable, can you heal them?" he asked.

"How have you shifted in your theological positions and spirituality over time?" he asked.

If there are truly excellent answers to any of these questions that can be delivered in less than thirty seconds, I'd like to hear them.

"I've shifted a lot in terms of how I act and interact with

people," I said in response to the last of these questions. "I think, I hope, that I've gotten a lot better at asking questions, at being genuinely curious and accepting of where people are at. I have more questions and far fewer answers."

Los Angeles – Accra – Washington, D.C. – Sydney – Zagreb – South Bend – Nairobi – San Diego – Atlanta – Madang – Kona – Canberra – London – Baltimore – Itonga – Vancouver – Harare – **Dushanbe** – **Lira** – **Petats** – Port Moresby – Brisbane – Ballina – Malibu

HOPE CHASES US

AS MIKE AND I continued to email each other throughout December while we waited to hear whether he would be granted leave from work to come to Australia, Mike also – one country at a time – systematically sent me all the mass emails he had sent out during the previous five years. There were about forty of them. He had several years' worth of my monthly essays. I guess he figured fair was fair.

These earlier emails weren't written to me, but I pored over them just as carefully as I read his current ones. I knew the broad details of where he'd been, what stuck with him, and how he talked about it all now – that showed up fairly clearly in our give-and-take. What I didn't know was how Mike had felt and reacted in the pressure cooker of *then*. How he'd gotten from there to here. Who he *had* been, not just who he was now.

This story mattered, I knew. It would provide clues to how Mike might cope with the pressure cookers of a future I was starting to sense just might be a possibility.

Dushanbe, Tajikistan

AROUND THE SAME TIME that I was drinking myself to sleep on the couch at night, wondering where my faith had gone and asking myself whether I'd made a mistake in moving to Los Angeles, Mike was wondering what, exactly, he was doing in Tajikistan.

"Once upon a time there was a young man named Mike," began one of these mass emails, written almost six months after Mike first set foot in Tajikistan. "Mike enjoyed traveling around the world spending time in various countries. He easily befriended people from different cultures. He learned languages quickly. Then one day Mike came to a place called Tajikistan. Now there's a different Mike."

In his own words, Tajikistan *broke* Mike.

He arrived outgoing, passionate about development work, and so eager to embrace the language and the culture that he moved in with a Tajik family.

It wasn't one thing that broke him; it was many. It was the complete lack of privacy, the squat toilets, spotty electricity, revolting food, and cold brown water. It was the fact that it was so frigid during winter that he had to wear five layers of clothes to the office. It was spending much of his time being sick with giardia and other nasty ailments. It was serving as the engineering expert on a seismic awareness project when all the technical materials were in Russian. But more than anything else, far more, it was his failure to live up to his own ideals and expectations regarding what the work should be, how it should be done, and how he should live while doing it.

Six months after arriving in the country, Mike hit bottom.

He didn't like Tajikistan, he didn't like the Tajiks, he didn't like himself, and he had a hernia that needed surgery. During the six weeks that he had to spend in Australia over Christmas having that surgery, he realized that he couldn't continue to live as he had been. When he returned to Tajikistan he moved out of shared housing and into a small flat. He reported in his emails that he was trying to be less consumed by his job. He was going on more hikes, he wrote, and had learned to unwind at the end of the day by listening to music.

Mike had enough determination to finish out the last six months of his contract, enough sense to leave at that point, and enough honesty to lay himself bare to faraway friends.

"For the rest of my days, I hope that my expectations of myself and my outlook upon life will be different," he wrote. "Part of me would still like to view myself as extraordinary, unbreakable, and indestructible. But I'm not. I'm flawed, weak. I'm ordinary. I've failed my own expectations of myself. Failed miserably."

But even after the beating Tajikistan had dished out, Mike also had enough spirit left to say, "I am profoundly grateful for these painful experiences. There are many things over which I have no or little control, but I can take specific actions to move in the direction that I want to travel in my life journey. And despite my weaknesses and limitations, I can offer love to fellow travelers I encounter along the way. Onward."

CONTINUING ONWARD TOOK MIKE next to northern Uganda to help provide water and sanitation facilities in camps for people driven from their homes because of a particularly vicious ongoing civil war. Eighteen months after that, Mike moved to Sri Lanka to help rebuild the tsunami-devastated coast.

Eighteen months after that, Papua New Guinea.

The transparent honesty I'd seen in Mike's early letters from Tajikistan continued, month after month, in these mass emails. From them, I learned that he loved Australia so much he'd applied for permanent residency in 2004 and just missed out. I learned that after his last girlfriend had called it off by phone while she was in Indonesia and he was in a hospital bed in Sri Lanka, he had only ever written of her circumspectly and graciously. I learned that he usually managed to hold light and dark together in the same letter.

I also saw some things in these letters that raised warning flags in my mind. Mike had been hospitalized three times in Sri Lanka for stress-related infections, and I recognized in his emails periodic episodes of burnout, with all its attendant self-questioning. How long could he keep doing this? Did he even want to anymore, anyway? Where had his early passion gone?

But I also saw Mike turn a clear lens on his struggles with a daily slog that was anything but glamorous and repeatedly search out moments of beauty, hope and humor in the midst of it all. I saw much to respect.

Lira, Uganda

DURING HIS STINT IN Uganda, Mike was shadowed for a week by a *National Geographic* photographer as he went about his work. When the issue came out, the online feature was titled *Hope in Hell: The reach of humanitarian aid*. One of the photos illustrating this article features Mike. In it, he is a six-foot-tall white beacon surrounded by dozens of children all reaching for him. He has his arm out, passing something into one of the waiting hands while scores of others clutch at him. The sea of cupped palms is very dark against the pristine blaze of his

T-shirt, and Mike's expression is difficult to read. His eyes are fixed on the one hand he's grasping, but his forehead is lined, his eyebrows tipped up toward each other in a small, worried salute.

Representing hope in hell did not look like an easy gig.

"I've been circling back to this topic of hope a lot lately, but I haven't even come close to figuring it out," I wrote to Mike in early December, shortly after returning from Vancouver and reading his letter about the *National Geographic* article.

"What is hope?" I wrote. "Can hope exist independently of something to place that hope in, some larger external source, or framework? Joy seems simpler to me, and being joyful in life is something I feel I have a better handle on than being hopeful. But hope – it's a puzzle. Attached to this letter is an unpublished essay called *Hope Chases Us* about an anti-trafficking benefit dinner I attended earlier this year."

Los Angeles, USA

HOPE CHASES US

WHAT DO YOU WEAR when you're going to spend the evening learning about sex slavery?

This was only one of the many important questions in life that I didn't have a good answer for on Saturday. Two hours before I was due at a benefit dinner for International Justice Mission, I was staring into my closet at a loss.

A black dress and boots doesn't work. I love these boots. They're the most extravagant pair of shoes I've ever bought – knee-high, buttery, black leather with mini-stiletto heels. But leather-clad calves and dark draped curves feel too vamp to me. A suit and jacket seems too clinical. What I really want to wear, jeans, is too casual. In the end I go for international eclectic – a blue cotton shirt from India over black pants, embroidered platform shoes from Malaysia, and a silver Orthodox cross from Ethiopia...

It's been two hundred years since the first abolition act was passed that made it unlawful for British subjects to capture and transport human beings, yet there are still about twenty five million people in the world today who are being held as slaves. That's almost twice the number trafficked from Africa during the entire four hundred years of the transatlantic slave trade. The buying and selling of people is now the world's second-most lucrative illegal profession, outranked only by the global trade in illegal arms.

Twenty five million is a number so large it defies comprehension. It's more than the entire population of Australia. Who are they, and where?

They are Cambodian men trafficked to Thailand to work on construction projects. They are Yemeni children smuggled into Saudi Arabia to work as street beggars. They are children from Mali working on cocoa plantations in the Ivory Coast.

To bring this slightly closer to home, the Ivory Coast holds forty-three percent of the world's market in cocoa, and the USA is the world's largest chocolate consumer.

To bring it closer still, the U.S. government estimates that about fifty-thousand women and children are trafficked into the United States every year for sweatshop labor, domestic servitude, or the sex trade.

...I pull up behind a shiny Corvette at the Millennium Biltmore and hand my keys to the valet. I am ashamed that after several recent stints in airport parking lots my car is filthy, and then proud that I do not own a Corvette. I'm ashamed, again, at the self-righteousness I recognize shadowing this thought. Then I am proud of my own humility.

I am only distracted from these mental gymnastics by the

grandeur of the hotel lobby – acres of marble, ornate columns, and gilded ceilings...

The program that I am handed as I enter the event informs me that, for this evening at least, I am a 17-year-old girl named Panida from a hill tribe in Thailand. When I was twelve, my family sent me off with a man who visited my village and promised that if I came to work in his cigarette factory my earnings would be enough to support the rest of the family. He lied. I ended up in a brothel, where I worked for three years before I was rescued.

...I sip an apple martini. It is cold and sweet against my glossed lips – the bite of spirits cloaked by gentle green. A maraschino promise glows red from the bottom of the glass. I wonder whether Panida likes martinis. Then I remember she's still too young to drink...

The walls of the ballroom are lined by carved pillars. An enormous chandelier hangs like an inverted wedding cake from the ceiling, four tiers of crystal falling toward the floor like a ballet of raindrops. At our table there doesn't seem to be enough space for all the cutlery and accoutrements: two wine glasses, bread, individual pats of butter, our own personal dessert platters, and salads of braised pears and honeyed pecans.

Staff member from International Justice Mission mount the stage. They speak of modern-day slavery with a facility honed by years of witnessing what generally happens when power operates for too long in an accountability vacuum. Laws are just words on paper, the speakers say, until they are made reality in the lives of the vulnerable. And the vulnerable are just statistics until there are faces and stories to put to the violations.

Grainy black-and-white footage of brothel raids taken from hidden surveillance cameras is projected onto a large screen behind the stage. We see dozens of Panidas in seedy rooms, awaiting customers. A ragged toy perched neatly on a bed is a heartbreaking symbol of one little girl's attempt to preserve some tattered remnant of a stolen childhood.

...Dessert taunts me all through dinner and in the end I don't know which to start with. The small round of raspberry cheesecake, the brandy-snap basket filled with cream and strawberries, or the chocolate truffle? My carefully chosen black pants feel too tight...

It is too easy to simply showcase the irony of dining on steak and chicken while these videos play. Too easy to only raise an eyebrow at the fact that a mere twenty-one percent of my expensive ticket for the event actually went to the charity. But I am reminded of a familiar biblical admonition to look first to the log in my own eye. I am the one who owns so many clothes that I can spend half an hour deciding what to wear. I am the one with enough disposable income to afford the ticket in the first place. And I'm now the one responsible for how I respond to the information that's being served to me on a silver platter right alongside three types of dessert.

The statement that catches me most off guard during the night is spoken near the end of the evening. It isn't the shocking statistic that the trafficking of women and children for sex brings in more money annually than the entire Microsoft empire. It's just six brave words.

"Hope chases us in this work."

During the last eight years of my life – in prisons, in orphanages for abused children, in villages gutted by war and studded with landmines – I'd been granted glimpses into lives where cruelty, desperation, and grief had become normal. If you look too deep into the heart of that reality for too long, it is profoundly overwhelming. Over time it's easy for cynicism to become a habit, even a refuge. It is tempting to rest in the numb embrace of a fatalistic paralysis.

...*That night I dream of Rwanda, a place I haven't yet been. After the benefit dinner I was up until one reading a book with the unforgettable title of* Emergency Sex and Other Desperate Measures. *I know better than to read this sort of stuff late at night. The tale is as raw as the title – three former U.N. workers detailing the savaging of their humanitarian ideals by successive missions to conflict zones. Their increasingly desperate disenchantment as the story unfolds is mesmerizing and excruciating, and the dreams this story grants me are black and white and full of mass graves and machetes...*

Hope chases us.

Sometimes it seems that hope could do with a lengthy course of steroids. Perhaps then it might stand a fighting chance in the footrace with despair.

But on a good day I can be anchored by remembering the story of the good Samaritan. In the instant the Samaritan walked past the wounded man lying in the ditch, he was not being called to hire and train a police force to escort travelers, hunt down the brigands and see them bought to trial (complete with defense attorneys) or single-handedly transform the entire Jericho road into a bastion of safety. He is lauded because he stopped to help the one.

My namesake for the evening, Panida, had lived within the borders of Thailand her entire life, but because she came from a hill-tribe minority group, she had never been recognized as a citizen. Two years after she was rescued from the brothel she finally received a Thai passport and, with it, some legally defensible rights. Her smile as she was pictured holding up her passport spilled joy and hope into a ballroom eight thousand miles from where she lived – hope that it is worth trying to make a difference one life at a time.

I've been in California this past week, not the brothels of Thailand or the hills of Rwanda. Stopping for one wasn't climbing into the ditch to haul out the wounded, rescuing a Panida, or picking up a scalpel. It was meeting a friend for breakfast, returning a phone call, and writing a check.

Cynicism is the wide path of least resistance, and hope never seems to find me when I'm on that track. But when I'm most often surprised by hope's companionship is also not when I'm trotting full speed down the road to Jericho. It's when, by my all-too-human standards, I'm not really making much progress at all.

It's when I pause to see others' love in action, helping liberate people from slavery and its usual breeding ground, poverty.

When I've stopped for beauty – flowers, music, mountains, sunsets, great stories, amazing food, and the peaceful hush of a summer evening.

And when I've stopped for one.

Mike, Papua New Guinea

"HOPE CHASING US," MIKE wrote to me the next day. "What a beautiful, precious image. Thanks for the reminder about guarding against cynicism.

"Why didn't you publish that one? I really like how you didn't cheapen it into the standard 'I feel guilty because of all the ironies' essay. I found the ending a bit abrupt, but I don't know how I'd end it."

Lisa, USA

"I HAVEN'T PUT IT on my website yet because I suspect I can

sell it, but I haven't gotten around to editing it again before I try." I wrote back the next night.

"And I'm not sure about the ending, frankly. It's interesting that you said it was abrupt. My main problem with it is that I'm not entirely sure I understand or mean what I've written in those last couple of lines. I know they're beautiful and all. But do I *really* feel hope when I've stopped for one? Or am I more often feeling impatient because my schedule's been thrown off, or helpless because I'm not sure how to help that one, or simply feeling ... nothing ... because I'm looking too far forward and haven't stopped to notice the moment?"

"I love the image of hope chasing us, love it. But putting into words what that actually means for me – that's different. I think I partially succeeded in that essay, but only partially."

Mike, Papua New Guinea

"DO YOU FEEL CHASED by hope?" Mike replied. "I don't most times. But I think that sometimes hope sneaks up on us when we're wallowing in a dark, dark place and bursts into the room holding a giant candle and says, 'Surprise! You forgot about me. But I haven't forgotten you!'

"I think I'm a fairly hopeful person, or at least an optimistic person. I even like to think of myself as a passionate person. I definitely used to be. Am I now? If I'm doing things that I (passionately) believe in, why am I so bloody tired half the time and so blah about life the other half? And does passion matter in comparison with, say, consistency?

"Passion. I think it's a double-edged sword. I'm trying to learn to wield it without inflicting too much harm on others or myself. Add this to the rolodex of things we can chat about in person someday. Hopefully sooner rather than later."

Lisa, USA

"PASSION IS ANOTHER PUZZLE, isn't it? I was driving home from work tonight and listening to Josh Groban's *O Holy Night* on the radio. That's probably my favorite Christmas song, and I think Groban's got a good voice, but his rendition was all carefully controlled technical perfection. It came across completely devoid of passion and didn't stir me in the slightest. How *can* you sing that song, with his talent, without throwing yourself heart and soul into it?

"But even as I point fingers at Groban I wonder about lack of passion in my own life. Maybe it's just natural that a keen awareness of not living up to our own expectations in many areas, including living passionately, sharpens as we get older. But I remain puzzled as to how the deep passions that I know I am capable of and the immense gratitude that I feel for so many blessings in my life can sometimes co-exist with a gray fog that can descend so completely some days that my head and my heart don't seem connected at all and I feel as if I'm wandering around wrapped in cotton wool.

"I wonder, even as I write this, whether hope or joy is connected more intimately with passion. What role does hope have in sustaining passion, or the other way around?

"It's almost midnight here now. Travis came home just as I finished writing that last bit.

"Sigh.

"Have I told you about Travis? That when I came back from Turkey in August he believed he was starring in his own reality TV show?

"I *thought* it was a passing thing, but yesterday we actually got some time to hang out together for the first time in weeks and those delusions are all still there, probably even more firmly entrenched. Travis is convinced that he's got the whole conspiracy figured out and it's driving him crazy (no pun intended) that no one will admit to any of it.

"I'm so glad I'm going to San Diego tomorrow to spend Christmas with Erica and Leah and the gang. I'm not incredibly freaked out like I was the first time Travis dumped this story on me, but I know I can't quite trust anything with regard to him at the moment. The whole situation breaks my heart. What would it be like to really believe that, to live under all that manufactured mental pressure? And how will he cope when this whole grand delusion that's giving his life purpose and meaning at the moment (even as it's putting him under incredible pressure) comes crashing down around him?

"It makes me feel helpless because I cannot see any way to reach him. And it makes me frustrated because I know I'm going to have to move out when I get back from Australia and the prospect of *that* is just exhausting. And, in the short term, it makes me incredibly unsettled when he's around, because I'm never quite sure what he'll do or say, or what mood he's in, and I can feel the mental and emotional turmoil that he's going through coming off him in waves.

"And yet, in the middle of all of this, there are glimpses of the flatmate I really enjoyed living with for the first year and a half.

"As I was yawning and making it clear I needed to go to bed tonight, he told me that he was journaling about all this and that he was going to write a book.

"'You'd better write nice things about me. You're going to make me famous,' I joked, trying to finish the conversation on a light note.

"'No,' he said to me, laughing. 'You'll make yourself famous. I'll just make you more famous.'

"It's late, Mike, and I have a throbbing headache. I must close and try and go to sleep."

Mike, Papua New Guinea

"IT'S CHRISTMAS EVE, LATE afternoon, and I'm stuck in the office waiting for my staff to return from all their personal errands around town. I'm going to be the mean manager who locks the project vehicle up at my house over Christmas break so that staff don't waste fuel donors intended for travel out to the projects on scuttling their friends around.

"Sorry to hear about what's going on at home. You totally need to move out. You already know that, so my saying it is only affirmation. In the meantime I hope that San Diego and good friends have cured your headache. Probably safe mental space is doing wonders. I hope.

"I hope I'm able to make it to Australia next month.

"I hope I can get better at managing my emotions. I hope passion will remain a healthy force in my life that spurs love.

"That last is an up-and-down journey. Today is down. I learned yesterday that a raiding party looted and destroyed some buildings in one of the villages where we're working. They also happened to destroy three of the precious seven toilets that my team has actually managed to get constructed there during the past three months. Ahh yes, just another day at work. These are the types of things that humanitarian organizations don't mention in their glossy adverts.

"(For the love of God, why did they choose to destroy the toilets?)

"On days like these I must remind myself that this is just a down and that ups exist, too, so I'm sending along a piece called *Jesus Wants You to Build a Toilet* that I wrote earlier this week about a day recently that made me feel passionate, and purpose-filled, and hopeful.

"It's well after the time I wanted to leave the office. The guys aren't back with the vehicle yet, so I'm faced with the decision of whether to stay or go home and hope for the best. It's Christmas Eve, though, and I'm leaning toward hope. And trust.

"Merry Christmas to you."

Mike, Petats, Papua New Guinea

JESUS WANTS YOU TO BUILD A TOILET

"JESUS WANTS YOU TO build a toilet for the women," I told Pastor Barry in my best broken Tok Pisin. Normally I feel a bit annoyed when people make Jesus the poster child for their personal cause. I remember, for example, the billboard in Atlanta a few years ago that showed a picture of a cherubic Jesus and said "Jesus was a vegetarian." I laughed every time I saw it.

But Pastor Barry wore a baseball cap that sported the phrase "Jesus is my boss," so I figured this might get his attention.

We were sitting on a bamboo bench on Petats Island, in Papua New Guinea. A refreshing sea breeze rustled the coconut palms and mango trees. The bright red hibiscus flowers danced in the wind. It was a beautiful Pacific morning – a perfect day for conducting an evaluation of the water and sanitation project we were implementing in the region.

I had just inspected one of the new ventilated improved pit toilets built near the church. It's a really well-constructed toilet. And Pastor Barry keeps a lock on it. The women told me it's only used on Sundays or special occasions. Apparently Pastor Barry doesn't want people to use it regularly. So most of the time people go in the bush or walk into the sea, but sometimes they get to use the nice new toilet.

I asked the women whether they liked it. They giggled, perhaps on account of my broken Tok Pisin, and perhaps because they were embarrassed that a white man with notebook, camera and funny GPS unit strung around his neck was asking them whether they like defecating in the lone toilet. After the initial embarrassment, the eyes of one of the women lit up. "Yes," she told me. "We feel safe with the toilet."

The United Nations has proclaimed this year the International Year of Sanitation. That may seem irrelevant for those of us who are able to flush and forget, but roughly a third of the people on the planet don't have access to improved sanitation. That more or less means two billion people relieve themselves in the bush.

Lack of improved sanitation has all sorts of negative effects on public health. Like dead children – diarrhea is still the leading cause of death for children under five. Like the additional burden for mothers who regularly have to take care of sick children. Like cholera outbreaks – ever hear of cholera occurring in a place with improved sanitation? Nope.

Sanitation is a basic human need. If you look at the data from New York, London, and Paris from the days before those cities had built sewers, you'll see that their mortality rates were about the same as mortality rates today in sub-Saharan Africa. Everybody poos. And in many places around the world, still, everybody poos on the open ground.

I've spent much of my time overseas focusing on improving access to clean water and sanitation. Women in displacement camps in northern Uganda, for example, would often wait in line for two hours to pump water, while about 1,500 schoolchildren would have to share two toilets. So we drilled more wells and built more toilets. In Sri Lanka, after the tsunami destroyed thousands of houses, we installed hundreds of wells and built hundreds of toilets in addition to rebuilding schools, health clinics, and homes.

In Papua New Guinea I've begun focusing more on improving hygiene practices than building infrastructure. We can build lots of toilets, but what if people don't actually use them? (Happens more often than you may think.) And if people don't wash their hands after using the toilet, it's likely there will be hardly any improvements in health.

So for the past year, my focus has been on behavior change: improving hygiene practices that complement improvements in infrastructure. But while assessing this project, I've been particularly moved by something that isn't directly related to safe water or improved sanitation.

Before our project, the women walked an hour or more to get water. To relieve themselves, they walked far into the bush or the mangroves. The women told us they used to be sexually assaulted by men hiding in the bush. Now that there are water taps and toilets close to their homes, they no longer get attacked on trips to fetch water or go to the toilet.

Domestic and sexual violence against women is prevalent in the Pacific. I reckon that women tend to get the short end of the stick all around the world, but it seems to me to be particularly bad here. In the Pacific, the women are damn lucky if they get any of the stick at all, because most of the time the men take the stick and beat them with it. Given a choice, I reckon I'd prefer to be a woman in Afghanistan than a woman in Papua New Guinea.

On Petats, the women told me that they felt safe when they used the new toilet.

"You know the Bible and I know the Bible," I said to Pastor Barry. "You know that Jesus loved the mamas and he loved the weak and the vulnerable. I think Jesus wants you to build a toilet

for the women."
    I hope he will.

Los Angeles – Accra – Washington, D.C. – Sydney – Zagreb – South Bend – Nairobi – San Diego – Atlanta – Madang – Kona – Canberra – London – Baltimore – Itonga – Vancouver – Harare – Dushanbe – Lira – Petats – **Port Moresby** – Brisbane – Ballina – Malibu

Pouring Sunshine and Rain

There's a chemical in your brain
It's pouring sunshine and rain.
You can never know what to expect
You're manic, manic
(Plumb, *Manic*)

Los Angeles, USA

WHILE MIKE AND I were busy writing emails and wondering about hope and passion, my family and our mutual friends were starting to see the odd public exchange on Facebook that made them wonder about us.

My parents put out the first feelers, and they were remarkably unruffled when I informed them that I had invited "that Mike guy I've been emailing" to come make himself at home with us for ten days during our family holidays.

"Well, I'm sure that'll be lovely for him," my mother said with a commendable lack of questioning or histrionics. "If he's been living in Papua New Guinea he probably needs a holiday somewhere nice, anyway."

"Yeah, I think he does," I said, trying to sound as if concern for this poor overworked email buddy in PNG was all that had motivated me to issue an invitation.

As the weeks slipped past and the date of my trip to Australia drew closer, however, my parents' restraint on this topic started to fray. It started with the odd inquiry as to how Mike was doing, and then it turned into one sort of query or another during every phone call. None of these queries, mind you, ran anything along the lines of "Are you sure you know what you're doing?" or "Are you out of your mind?" On the contrary, my parents appeared to be most nervous that Mike might have a sudden change of heart and decide not to come after all.

"How's Mike?" Mum asked me one night shortly after Christmas. "What's up with his plans for January?"

"Oh, yeah," I said, distracted because I was trying to finish something on the computer and talk at the same time despite the fact that I regularly scolded Mum for that very practice. "We were emailing about this the other day. There's this big meeting in Port Moresby in the middle of January—"

"Awww," Dad interrupted me. "He can't come then?"

"Oh, no," I hastened to reassure them. "It looks like he's going to make it for at least a week. Maybe more. And assuming we're getting on and haven't freaked out during the first two days, we might both go to Melbourne together that last weekend, too. It's not quite sorted."

Dad sounded thrilled. "Oh, that's good then. He knows there's going to be a whole bunch of other people here, too?"

Oh, that's right, I remembered. Not only would my brother

and his now-fiancée be there, as well as my sister and niece, but so would the six other friends we had collectively invited north for the Australia Day long weekend.

"He'll be fine," I said. "I think he's pretty ... adaptable."

"That's great!" Mum said. "He'll have a great time. It'll be very relaxing. Tell him we're glad he's coming."

"Okay," I said.

"Make sure you tell him, okay?"

"Mum, okay! I'll tell him."

THE FIRST OF OUR mutual friends to question me about Mike was Shelly, younger sister of my first crush, Paul. I'd tutored Shelly in French when she was nine and I was sixteen. Shelly had somehow managed to learn how to speak French fluently in spite of me. She was now a doctor, living in Melbourne.

"Hey Lis, how's things with your new friend, Mike Wolfe??" Shelly emailed me out of the blue with characteristic directness. "Seems you two get along pretty well."

"Shells, you rascal," I wrote back without addressing her question. "You've just swung the door wide open for some reference-checking. So, do you want to send me ten words or phrases that describe our mutual friend Mr. Mike?"

"Reference-checking, ay?" Shelly replied. "Well those of us in Melbourne who know you both commented on it a little while ago, and we thought it good. Ten words or phrases, hmmm:

"1. talkative

"2. thoughtful

"3. fun

"4. kind

"5. real

"6. integrity

"7. out there

"8. energetic

"9. compassionate

"10. and again, talkative

"So, what's the story, my friend....?" she finished.

"There is no 'story' yet," I wrote back. "But there is probably what I would call 'potential to be a story.' It is rather hard to judge story potential when you've never met face-to-face. Hence, reference checking. So feel free to send any additional thoughts, lists, or formal reference letters my way. If this made a family dinner conversation on your end and was pronounced good, then the story potential just went up a notch. There is, however, a lot of space for notches between L.A. and PNG."

AFTER MY EXCHANGE WITH Shelly I decided that reference checking might actually be a good idea, so I wrote to Ryan.

In the three years since I'd visited him in Vancouver, Ryan had moved to Pakistan. There he'd fallen in love with Pakistani woman named Celestina and married her. Canadian officials hadn't exactly proved overeager to recognize the marriage and issue Celestina residency papers, so as the earthquake-relief programs they were working on began to wind down, Ryan and Celestina moved to Liberia to work and wait out the slow grind of Canada's immigration processes.

Ryan had not been writing nearly enough essays for my liking, something I harassed him about via email every couple of months. It was easy enough to slip a casual query onto the end of a note.

"I can't write more now," I wrote. "Am running late, and this week is stacking up in advance of heading to Australia in two weeks. I'll be spending some significant time there with another friend of yours, Mike Wolfe. You worked together in Afghanistan, didn't you? Did you get on? Impressions? I'm curious, and there's potential (nothing more at this stage, but potential is a good start) that it could be more than a passing interest."

"I met him years ago in Afghanistan and we've bantered back and forth with bits of writing and aid-worker angst," Ryan replied. "He seems much more suited to development work, judging from the flavor of his recent writing. Maybe because in development you work on a smaller scale but see real change if you see it at all – unlike relief work, where you work on a large scale and wonder constantly if you are making any difference at all other than to your own life. Anyway, all that to say, I think he's a good person to have potential with."

THIRD-PARTY ENCOURAGEMENT FROM AUSTRALIA and Liberia was all well and good, but I spent much of the last two weeks before I got onto the plane to Australia wondering whether Mike and I were even going to get the chance to explore this potential. For as the new year ticked over, things started to go wrong on both sides of the Pacific.

At my place in California, things went from bad to worse very quickly after Christmas.

Now that we'd broached the topic of the reality show again, Travis was like an uncorked bottle of warm champagne, fizzing over every time I came near him. Nothing seemed to help. Letting him talk for hours about his delusions got us nowhere; he just got progressively more worked up as he explained it to me over and over again – improbable scenario stacked upon improbable scenario that he had somehow fashioned into story and then forged into desperate conviction.

He *was* starring in this reality TV show, he kept insisting. We *were* all in on it. Why couldn't *someone* just tell him the truth?

By early January I made exactly zero progress convincing Travis that he wasn't autistic, that our house was probably not bugged, and that I definitely wasn't his pathologically deceptive co-star in a reality television program. I was also no closer to convincing him that he'd suffered some sort of psychotic break and was in rather desperate need of psychiatric care.

I'd talked to some of Travis' family, but they were just as overwhelmed as I was. He refused to see a psychiatrist and we couldn't force him. He couldn't be involuntarily hospitalized unless we could prove him a danger to himself or others, and the closest Travis had come to this was holding a knife to his wrists in the kitchen one night.

He was begging me to level with him, talking about the pressure he was feeling knowing that everyone was watching him all the time, when he suddenly reversed the angle of the knife he was using to chop vegetables and held the blade against his arm.

"If I did a good enough job," he challenged me across the kitchen bench, "you could never get the ambulance here in time."

"You're probably right," I said, gambling on my instinctive sense that he wasn't serious, not yet. "So please don't. That would really mess up my evening plans."

Without a more obvious threat I knew that the police could, at most, only hold him for three days anyway, not nearly long enough for most antipsychotic drugs to really kick in.

I was stuck. And seven days before I was supposed to fly to Australia I was *done*.

———— ∞∞ ————

THAT NIGHT I UNSUCCESSFULLY tried to head off yet

another three-hour conversation with Travis by playing one of
the few trump cards I thought that he, being a writer himself,
would respect.

"I need to write tonight," I told him long before we finished
eating dinner together. After dinner was done, I started moving
around the kitchen, stacking the dishwasher, deliberately giving
off "I'm preoccupied" signals.

"Will you sit down?" Travis said, irritated. "It's very difficult
to talk to you when you're messing with other things."

"I need to go work," I said.

Normal cues didn't work that night. I had to interrupt him
several times to remind him that I had other plans. Finally I had
to tell him that I was going to walk away now, that we'd talk
more about this later.

Undeterred, Travis followed me upstairs, stood in the door of
my bedroom, and continued talking. Five minutes later he hadn't
paused for breath and I had to interrupt him again.

"Look," I said, willing my voice not to shake. "I am *not*
going to talk about this with you anymore right now. I can't see
any productive way that we can have this conversation. I've told
you that I believe you're temporarily paranoid. There's nothing
that I can say right now that's going to convince you that you
don't have autism. There's nothing that you can say right now
that will convince me that you do. And, *I have to work!*"

Travis looked at me, startled, and left.

I sat there, shaking, trying to catch my breath, knowing that
whatever else I was going to do that night I was wrecked for any
productive writing.

Two minutes later, before I'd decided what on earth I *was*
going to do when I certainly wasn't going to come out of my
bedroom for the rest of the evening, Travis called up from
downstairs with just a hint of sheepish in his tone.

"Do you want a glass of wine? I probably owe you one."

"Yes, you do," I called out, not feigning how much I suddenly *did* want a glass of wine. But as I heard the cork come out downstairs and the wine gurgle into the glasses, I suddenly wondered …

Would he ever put anything in it? He still believed someone had slipped something into his drink in Vegas months ago – would he ever do something similar? Was he just play-acting calm? Was he angry that I'd shut him down? As I took a deep breath and told myself not to be ridiculous, I also wondered whether paranoia was catching.

When he bought the wine up he offered up a toast.

"To this next year being the best year for both of us," he said. "And to me overcoming my autism, and my paranoia."

He had spoken in desperate jest, but I offered up a silent and hearty "Amen. Please let it be so."

I drank the wine as a small, silent statement of faith that he would not hurt me. Then I shut my door, feeling sick to my stomach, and wrote a long, anguished letter to Mike called *Tonight's washing machine of negative emotions.*

"It's such a mixture of stuff," I wrote after I'd described the evening. "I'm so sad because I'm watching someone who I know well and care for deeply spiraling down this slide of paranoia and I can't do anything to get in the way. I can see further than he can, and all I see at the bottom of this slide is depression and worse. And despite what I said to him tonight, when he drew breath long enough to ask for my professional opinion (again), despite the fact that I was so careful to place the word *temporary* in front of the word *paranoid*, I don't know if it *is* actually temporary now.

"I knew I should not expect to be able to talk him out of his delusions, but knowing the theory is one thing. Seeing it in a client is one thing. Seeing it in someone you know well – that's another thing entirely. But I'm supposed to be a psychologist, for crying out loud. How could I not have seen this coming? However you look at it, if anyone should be able to get in the way of this and break his fall, it should be me and I'm failing. I am failing in this. I know that may be an impossible task, and it isn't really my (quote) responsibility (unquote) to save him anyway. But to some extent it is, you know. Because you don't get much closer a neighbor to love than your flatmate."

But as I sat in my room that night writing to Mike about the whole mess, I knew that I was effectively about to abandon Travis to his battle. With the sound of pouring wine had come the realization that I was starting to doubt my own judgment. That I was losing my grip on this situation, if I had ever had one to begin with. That I needed to move out as soon as possible.

Port Moresby, Papua New Guinea

IN PAPUA NEW GUINEA, meanwhile, Mike was trying to wrap up his work before taking time off and mourning being robbed for the third time in a month.

When he'd been in the Solomon Islands four weeks earlier, his favorite pair of shoes had been stolen off the porch of someone's house while he was inside having dinner. As he only owned about three pairs of shoes, this was no small loss, and he'd immediately ordered another pair and had them shipped to me so that I could bring them to Australia and hand them off. I still had no idea how tall Mike was, but after his new shoes arrived, I did know that he had size thirteen feet.

After the shoe incident, however, the thefts became more serious.

During the Christmas party that Mike threw at his house,

two people were robbed of their bags, wallets, and keys, and one person was knifed while trying to retrieve them. Mike described it this way in a letter:

"Bobby was able to find the boys. He got the keys back, at least. They knifed him. I brought him into my kitchen and washed out his knife wound and got my first-aid kit, then I called for Laurence because he's a doctor and I'm not. Laurence said it's a long wound, but shallow. Bobby will be okay. We washed it out and bandaged him up. I gave him another beer. At 1 a.m. after everyone leaves I'm still buzzing and unable to sleep. I take a Valium."

"Well, you know what they say," I wrote back the next day, "A Christmas party isn't a Christmas party if it doesn't involve a stabbing and end with Valium."

On January 1st Mike was in Port Moresby and it was *his* turn to have a bag stolen – a bag containing his laptop, cash, his passport, immunization records, a GPS, an iPod, a digital camera, sunglasses, backup documents, and a copy of Salman Rushdie's *Midnight's Children*.

After a day spent driving around settlements and negotiating with the local hoodlums, known as *raskols*, four hundred dollars in "assistance fees" retrieved the computer, camera, GPS, flash drive, and sunglasses.

No passport. No iPod. No cash. No Salman Rushdie.

From our point of view, the most serious of these losses was the passport, since (as I learned the hard way several years before) you can't travel internationally without a valid one. Mike tried telling the gangs that the passport had an embedded computer chip in it and that the U.S. military could track down the people who'd stolen it.

"They can. They won't." Mike wrote to me. "I wonder if the raskols read my bluff?"

Figuring they probably had, Mike had immediately lodged a request for a new passport with the U.S. embassy in Port Moresby. He was promised it would arrive within two weeks. We crossed our fingers.

But six days before he was supposed to leave for Australia, Mike was still in Port Moresby and still without a passport, and when he rang his home base in Madang about a work matter, he learned he was now also without many of his remaining worldly possessions. Thieves had broken into his house again and looted it.

"I wonder what exactly they chose to take: what they deemed worthy of their dirty thieving paws," he wrote to me. "My books? My external hardrive that has the backup of all my files and all my pictures from the past four years? My yoga mat? My hiking shoes? My clothes? I left behind one pair of underwear in my top drawer so that I'd have a clean pair when I returned to Madang in February. I sure hope they didn't take that. I'm not so happy with PNG at the moment. It's only stuff. Stuff's not important. But it's annoying, dammit. See you in a week, hopefully. Hopefully I'll also make it through the next six days without losing too much more stuff."

"Shocker," I wrote. "I'm sorry. Is there anyone who could send you an inventory of what's still there so you at least know (particularly about the hard drive, oh, and the clean underwear – I would imagine those two are top of your priority list)? Maybe the next year is going to be the year of embracing solidarity with the poor in whole new ways for you. If the first twelve days of the year are anything to go by, trend analysis suggests that you will be robbed approximately 86 more times this year, in 86 different cities. Could be an exciting year."

Los Angeles, USA

WHEN I WASN'T AT work, I spent most of the week before
I left for Australia looking for a new place to live. I loved the
apartment that Travis and I shared, and I'd now lived there
longer than I'd lived anywhere else in my life, but I'd eventually
learned that when you don't feel entirely safe, it's hard to feel at
home, regardless of how you define it. Now I was just eager to
get out.

I knew without the shadow of a doubt that the Travis who
had moved in with me would never hurt me, but the Travis I was
now living with was not the Travis who'd moved in with me. I
could no longer completely trust that either logic or reality were
grounding his mind or guiding his actions. He was six inches
taller than me and stronger, and I couldn't even lock my bedroom
door. I didn't want to be, but I was scared – scared in a way I'd
rarely been overseas. The sort of jumpy scared that comes from
living with extended uncertainty.

My heart sank every time I drove into the garage and saw his
car in its space. Inside the apartment the floor was littered with
those proverbial eggshells. When we weren't talking about his
delusions, the mundane exchanges we did have about writing
projects, daily activities and weekend plans *seemed* relatively
normal, but they were shadowed by mutual suspicion. I could not
draw a deep breath.

I didn't go into or out of our place without my cell phone in
one pocket and my keys in the other, and when we were at home
at the same time, I watched. Probably the same wary, intent
watching that everyone else who'd heard the TV-show story was
employing. In one sense it was no wonder that he thought we
were all in on something without him.

We were.

Sanity.

Three days before I was supposed to leave for Australia I found a new place to live. It was a bit more than I'd wanted to pay, but I knew the minute I walked into the quiet one-bedroom apartment that it was perfect, and by the time I flew out I'd signed a lease and picked up the keys so that I could move in as soon as I got back – that very day, if need be. What I *hadn't* done was tell Travis that I was moving out.

I desperately wanted to sit down with him and lay it all out on the table, but I just couldn't bring myself to do it. No matter how I worried the puzzle in my head, I couldn't seem to make the different pieces fit into the same equation: to love Travis with transparent honesty and to make sure that I stayed safe when he seemed so volatile.

In the end I didn't tell him. Instead, I packed up my valuable possessions piecemeal and smuggled them out of the house, stowing them in the garage of my friend, Grace.

After my last trip to Grace's garage, the night before my flight, I went into the house to say a weary farewell to Grace and her two dogs. In bewilderingly short order, the new dog (half pit bull) decided that the old dog (half Great Dane) was getting more than his fair share of attention and attacked him.

By the time the dogs paused to take stock and Grace and I were able to grab one collar each, a truly remarkable amount of blood was sprayed across the walls, the carpet, and our clothes in spotty red arcs. The back seat of Grace's car didn't fare any better after we finally were able to manhandle the most grievously injured party (the new dog) into the vehicle to rush her to the animal hospital.

We had plenty of time to discuss the whole event during the three hours we sat in the emergency room holding a towel to the dog's neck.

"You told me," Grace said without any blame in her tone, "that Barnabus would be happier and less lonely if I got another dog."

"I meant a *puppy*, Grace," I said. "Not a ten-year-old half-pit-bull stray from the animal shelter." I glared down at the new dog that Grace had named Naomi. Despite the fact that blood was still dripping from her neck, Naomi looked perfectly content now that she had Grace's undivided attention.

"This is the third fight she's started in three weeks," I said. "You have to take her back."

"I know," Grace said and sighed deeply. "You know, you've been there for two of those fights…" She left the rest of the sentence hanging suggestively.

I maintained that I was merely an innocent bystander and that this altercation was not my fault. Grace, who was fully versed in the current events of my life, was not convinced. She posited, rather, that I was a drama-carrier – that I bred it wherever I went and that my mere presence had set the dogs off.

I wanted to be able to firmly refute this allegation.

I couldn't.

Los Angeles – Accra – Washington, D.C. – Sydney – Zagreb – South
Bend – Nairobi – San Diego – Atlanta – Madang – Kona – Canberra –
London – Baltimore – Itonga – Vancouver – Harare – Dushanbe – Lira
– Petats – Port Moresby – **Brisbane – Ballina** – Malibu

THE CHICKEN DANCE

Mike, Papua New Guinea

"GOOD MORNING, LISA," MIKE greeted me by email the
morning he was to fly to Australia.

"Monday morning," he wrote. "Yippee. Bags packed. Report
mostly finished. Brand new passport safely tucked away in
pocket. Just half a day left in the office and then I'm off to Port
Moresby Airport. Hopefully I'll be able to make it to the airport
without getting robbed. Yippee.

"Last night I had dinner alone. Me, my journal, thoughts, and
doubts. Oh my word, am I really doing this? Am I really about
to get on a plane and meet a special friend on the other end and
then spend two weeks at her house? Gulp. I mean, it seemed so
natural a few months ago. There was no hesitation at all then, no
doubts. She emails saying that she'll be home in January. I really

want to meet this interesting person who's begun to capture my heart. I ask whether it would be okay for me to come visit. … It was all so natural. No inhibitions, no fears.

"And last night … yikes. Doubt. Fear. Gulp.

"But now it's Monday morning. Adventure. I'm getting on a plane! I'm going to Australia! I'm going to meet Lisa! Whoo hooo! Adventure.

"So see you later today. If you're at all fearful that you might miss spotting me at the airport, just look for the guy who has clammy hands and sweat marks under his arms."

Lisa, Australia

AT THE SAME TIME that Mike was drafting the email above, I was writing one of my own to him.

"By now," I wrote, "I assume you're finished with the report – or very nearly – and starting to transition into holiday mode, and thinking about a couple of weeks off work, and the prospect of crashing at the home of someone you haven't met yet, and of three months of emails becoming flesh (most likely with less perfect results than were achieved the first time – or at least the most famous time – that word became flesh).

"And I'm starting to think about picking you up at the airport late this afternoon and hoping I recognize you, because I'm awful with faces (really, I am, it's almost clinical) and wondering what we are going to talk about for two and a half hours in the car on the way home.

"This, I realize, is quite a ridiculous thing to worry about. I suspect neither of us is particularly socially awkward most of the time, and I don't feel we lack for common ground. But there's something slightly jarring, although exciting, about switching gears from text to talk. I, for one, suspect that I'm more confident and more uninhibited in text land, but I suspect and hope that once we get past the initial weird zone we'll be fine.

"I expect the weird zone to last approximately 43 minutes, by the way.

"I just this minute got your email from this morning and laughed to see I'm not the only one wondering what we're doing and whether we are a little out of our minds.

"I am reminding myself that life is risk and that the worst thing that's going to happen is that you get a good holiday out of this and we cement a new friendship. That's not a bad worst. It's a risk worth taking, methinks.

"So I'll be there to pick you up this afternoon unless I get lost ... which is a distinct possibility. So if I'm not there, hang tight and I should get there eventually.

"See you this afternoon. I'm glad you're coming.

"P.S. I want it to be noted that I should not be held responsible for anything I might say or do in the weird zone, and I think we should postpone all first impressions until tomorrow."

Brisbane, Australia

I ARRIVED AT BRISBANE airport to pick Mike up more than an hour early. His plane hadn't even landed yet.

I'd brought a book with me but was totally unable to concentrate on it. In the end I left it open in my lap while I worked on a coffee one careful sip at a time and tried to think of something other than how nervous I was feeling.

The only things coming to mind, however, were *other* times I'd felt excruciatingly, tight-of-chest, short-of-breath nervous.

As a little girl, waiting to play the organ at a recital in the middle of a shopping mall.

The first time (and most times since then, really) I had to get up in front of a group and lead a workshop.

Other times I'd waited in airports, hopeful and scared, to greet strangers.

The first time I'd given a book reading.

Before the interview in Vancouver.

This train of thought was not helping. Neither was the caffeine in the coffee. I thought about what I'd written to Mike just that morning. Somewhere at the back of my mind I knew that all that stuff about risks worth taking was still true. But right then most of my mind (and all 2,037 of the acrobatic butterflies in my stomach) were running wild and free in the "are we both out of our minds?" territory.

I glanced up at the arrivals board again.

Beside the listing for Mike's flight, the status had just been updated from "On Schedule" to "Landed."

I stood up, tucking my book away and throwing the rest of my coffee into the trash. I knew it would probably be at least another thirty minutes before Mike cleared customs, but I couldn't sit still any longer. I found a spot across from the door that he would walk out of, leaned against a pillar, and started to scan every Caucasian male emerging from customs who looked somewhere between twenty and fifty.

Either men look at me far more than I usually notice or there was something strange about the intensity of my own scrutiny that day, because in the forty-five more minutes it took for Mike to walk out those doors, more than a handful of men caught my gaze and returned it with a direct and purposeful intensity of their own that I found very confusing.

"Is that him???" I would wonder, my heart rocketing up into my throat, as another man caught my eye and took a couple of steps in my direction. "No, wait, it can't ... maybe it is. ... No, I think Mike's hair is lighter than that. ... Why is he walking toward me? ... Okay, turning away. It's not him. Not him. Not him. Breathe."

By the time Mike actually appeared, I'd nearly hugged two strangers and I was pretty sure I was breaking out in hives.

I DID RECOGNIZE HIM. Or, more accurately, I recognized his smile. I saw that first, almost in isolation. Wide and open, it was reassuringly reminiscent of the tone of his letters.

He walked out of immigration smiling, wearing a red and white shirt and carrying a beat-up duffel bag and two duty-free bottles of wine.

We hugged hello and the top of my head slotted under his chin. He was tall, at least six feet. There were no sweat marks on his shirt. His hands weren't clammy. Mine were.

I can't remember our first words. I probably asked him how his flight was. I may not have been speaking in full sentences. The first words I actually remember us exchanging in person, about ninety seconds after we met, are these:

Mike: (grinning) "Weird zone's over."

Me: "You can't just unilaterally declare weird zone over. It's not over. I still have 41 minutes left."

Mike: "No, it's over. Can you hold the wine for a minute? I have to go to the bathroom."

EITHER MIKE WAS BETTER at acting or he was genuinely less nervous than I was, because the only time I saw him a little startled that day was when I handed him the keys to the car as we reached the parking lot and asked if he would drive back to Ballina.

"You want me to drive your parents' car?"

"I haven't driven much on this side of the road lately," I said. "You have."

"Okay." He took the keys and nodded, and I didn't have to tell him the other reasons I wanted him to drive: that I was worried I was too unfocused to be totally safe and that I wanted the chance to watch him.

So Mike drove and I sneaked glances, and in the dark cocoon of the car I slowly but surely started to calm down. There were no Disney fireworks or choirs of angels singing the Hallelujah Chorus or electric frissons of immediate sexual tension. What there *was* was ease.

We talked about the recent robbery of Mike's house.

"Any more information on what's missing?" I asked.

"No," Mike said. "But my boss has decided that that house is too unsafe for staff, so they're moving me out while I'm away."

We talked about first impressions and whether you *can* postpone them.

"Yes," Mike said. "I don't pay any attention to first impressions."

"It's impossible not to give first impressions any weight," I said. "We form them very quickly and almost unconsciously."

"They're unreliable," Mike said.

"Are they?" I asked. "I think they can be, but do you *really* think they are generally unreliable?"

We did *not* at that point talk about any first impressions we may have had earlier that afternoon. Instead we talked about Mike's new passport and how he was going to replace his work visa and my own recent work-visa interview at the U.S. consulate in Sydney and Travis.

"I moved my jewelry, my journals, and some of my clothes out of the house," I said. "I really don't think he would trash my stuff or anything like that, but I just can't be sure."

"How are you going to tell him?" Mike asked.

"I wrote to him yesterday and told him I'd be moving out shortly after I got back," I said. "I haven't heard anything from him yet, though."

Mike and I found all sorts of things to talk about without any trouble at all during that ride home. So many things, in fact, that we didn't get around to talking about my family – the family that he would shortly be meeting – until we were almost there.

"Is there anything in particular that I should know about your parents?" Mike asked as we pulled into the driveway of their house.

"Uh, no," I said, kicking myself for not having thought of this earlier. "Just be yourself."

Ballina, Australia

AS WE UNLOADED MIKE'S bags from the car and started toward the house, I was suddenly flooded with a new wave of nervousness. There were two main thoughts vying for airplay in my mind:

(1) There were lights on in that house. Mike was going to *look at me*.

(2) My parents and my little sister were in there waiting, no doubt dying to look him over. They'd done an excellent job of pretending casual and low-key all week, but I knew they were fiercely curious.

With regard to this second point, I couldn't figure out if I was more wary of something *they* might do or say, something *Mike* might do or say, or something *I* might do or say. I was just sure that there was definite wacky potential in the moment.

I was right. Within ten minutes of our arrival, the conversation had somehow led my mother to scamper off and retrieve her favorite speaking prop: the screaming rubber chicken.

A word about this chicken.

My mother is a talented public speaker. She can have a roomful of adults laughing within minutes of ascending the stage, and in the process she can get away with saying and doing the corniest and most ridiculous things without sacrificing any dignity.

Several years ago she stumbled across the screaming rubber chicken in a game store. It is the ugliest chicken you can imagine. Its squishy rubber body looks plucked and scrawny and has been unceremoniously dipped in bright yellow paint. When you squeeze it and let go it emits a horrible high-pitched shrieking – as if an insane cat is suffering a prolonged death. The harder you squeeze, the longer and more frantically the chicken wails.

My mother loves this chicken. She loves it so much that she went out shortly after she acquired hers and bought one for me to use when I present stress-management workshops.

"What am I supposed to do with that?" I had asked when she first presented me with my very own screaming rubber chicken.

Being faced with this query in response to a gift would dent most people. Not my mother.

"You can use it like this," Mum said, grinning. "When you're introducing the workshop you can say something like, 'Ever had a day when you feel like this?'" She gave the chicken a gentle squeeze and it moaned piteously. "Or what about a day when you feel like *this*?" She clutched the chicken slightly harder this time and the chicken complained more loudly. "*Or* what about a day when you *feel like this*?" She squeezed all the air out of the chicken's floppy latex belly and let go. The chicken screeched as if a tribe of small, wicked children had tied firecrackers to its tail feathers.

By this time both of my siblings, who had witnessed this whole gift exchange, were literally rolling on the floor. I think it was probably half the screaming rubber chicken and half the fact that *I* was *not* laughing.

"I am *not* using that chicken in my workshops, Mum," I said.

"Why not?" she asked. "It's perfect."

"Mum!" I said. "I'm already fighting an uphill battle. I am young and a woman, and I'm trying to teach disaster-relief workers about stress and trauma. If I bring out that chicken I will blow any respect points I have earned from having worked in jail and with the police and traveling solo around the Balkans. I do not yet have the years or the moxie to pull off that chicken during a workshop. I know my limits."

This was the chicken that my mother went to find the night I brought Mike home. Lo and behold, she came back with not one but *two* bright yellow chickens.

"Look," she said, holding up the new, fuzzy one. "I found a new chicken. Check it out!"

My mother closed her hands around the neck of this new chicken and it began to writhe in her grasp. Large, alarmed plastic eyes protruded from its head as if on springs, and a pointy red tongue shot out of its beak and fell sideways, limp.

I couldn't look at Mike, so I looked at my sister instead. Michelle was looking back and me and giggling with her hand over her mouth in that way that you laugh when you've just seen someone fall down a flight of stairs at the library with an armful of books. The way you laugh when you know you *shouldn't* be laughing.

We all admired the choking chicken routine for a moment, and then I let desperation and curiosity compel me to open my mouth – *someone* had to say something.

"What happens when you press that button?" I asked, pointing at the "Press here" button buried in the yellow feathers on the chicken's chest.

"I don't know," Mum said intrigued, "I've never done that. I didn't even know that was there."

As she touched the button, a familiar song started to play and the toy chicken, eyes wiggling maniacally, began to dance.

"The chicken dance!" Michelle and Mike exclaimed at about the same time.

"What's the chicken dance?" My mother asked, marveling at the new skill of this wondrous chicken.

"You've never seen the chicken dance?" Michelle asked.

"It goes like this!" Mike said, leaping up, sticking his hands in his armpits and starting to jump around the kitchen, singing.

"Come-on," Mike urged us.

Michelle, still giggling, apparently deciding that *she* had nothing to lose and joined in without hesitating.

I stood there for a second with the plate of leftovers I'd been warming up for Mike in my hand.

How exactly had we descended to the level of performing the chicken dance in a brightly lit kitchen in front of my parents within fifteen minutes of walking into the house?

Then I sighed, put the plate down, and joined in.

WHEN I CAME DOWNSTAIRS on the second morning of his stay, Mike was already up. He was sitting on the porch swing on the back deck, staring out across the cane fields and the river, out to the blue sweep of sea neatly hemmed by a ribbon of beach.

"Hi," he said.

"Hey," I said. "Where's everyone?"

"Your parents are around somewhere," he said. "Want some

coffee?"

"Please," I said, sitting down on the swing beside him. "Morning is not my time."

"I know," he said with a small sigh. "It's my time."

"I know," I said.

"I *don't* know what you take in your coffee, though," he said.

"Milk," I said. "One sugar."

He started to get up and paused.

"Lis," he said, "what are we going to do?"

It felt like he didn't really need an answer right then, but I answered anyway.

"We have time. We'll figure it out."

As Mike started to stand again, the screen door slid open and my mother stepped onto the deck.

"You two," she said to me.

"Yeah?"

"Your father and I are out tonight, so you can cook for yourselves, eat leftovers, or find some other option."

I looked at Mike.

"Do you want to go on a hot date tonight?" I asked him.

"Who with?" he said.

"Me," I said.

"Well then, how can I say no to that?"

AFTER DINNER THAT NIGHT I waited for Mike to kiss me. He never did.

We walked along the riverbank, licking our ice cream cones, until we found a free bench. We sat. I dripped chocolate down my white pants. I listened to the wind snap the flags above us against the poles. I shivered in the unseasonably cool breeze and wondered whether Mike would notice and put an arm around me to help keep me warm.

He didn't.

I thought about scooting over and kissing *him* but decided against it. The guy was in my country, at my house, and surrounded by my family and friends. The least I could do was respect his personal space.

Part of my brain was listening to what Mike was talking about, and another part was busy mulling over the question he had asked me that morning.

What were we going to do?

Our three months of emails had been flavored by friendly frankness that had strayed into barely perceptible flirting on only a handful of occasions. I guess I'd assumed that it would be different face-to-face – that if we were going to work, a different sort of energy would immediately enter the equation.

It didn't. Not that night. Not for the entire first week he was there. Not even during a classic and completely unscripted moment on day four when I took Mike to meet my grandparents.

That day my grandfather, cheerful and garrulous as always, talked at length about a documentary he'd just seen on crocodile farming in the Northern Territory and then pressed the DVD on us so that we could take it home and watch it ourselves. But it was my grandmother who was in particularly fine form. She served Mike tea in china teacups and delicious slices of cake, and somewhere in there she also served him the totally out-of-context and completely inaccurate statement (delivered with the utmost gravity) that I was "definitely going to adopt two black African babies very soon."

Mike looked at me, puzzled. I hadn't let him in on any adoption plans. In the moment, I could only smile and hope he understood that this was because *there weren't any*.

But I can't blame *all* the embarrassing moments that

occurred that afternoon on my grandparents. The last one was all me.

"Darling," my grandmother said, handing me three of my own books just as we were leaving, "can you sign these, please? One of them is ours and two are to give away."

I sat down the deck, twiddling the pen while I tried to figure out what to write inside my grandparents' book.

"What do you think," I began, looking up at Mike, who was standing in front of me. At that precise moment the pen flew out of my hands, up into the air, and straight down my cleavage like a guided missile.

Mike didn't say a word. His lips twitched, but he turned his head and looked out at the river while I, blushing, retrieved the pen from where it had lodged itself firmly in my bra.

That entire first week, Mike kept a maddeningly respectful distance. We went walking, we played board games, we spent hours and hours sitting on the porch swing together, talking. He didn't make a move. He didn't even *look* at me wrong. I started to wonder if he was even interested.

MORE THAN OUR FIRST kiss, more than any particular words, the real emotional landmark for me was the first time Mike reached for me.

We were on the porch swing talking, not of the letters that we had written to each other but of the ones we'd written before that: my essays and the five years' worth of mass emails he'd sent to me.

"What did you learn?" Mike asked, laughing, when I told him how carefully I'd combed through his old letters.

"I learned that I don't ever want to move to Tajikistan," I said.

Mike groaned at the reference to the toughest year of his life.

"Well, that proves that you don't need to experience something firsthand to learn a valuable lesson," he said.

We fell silent. Mike was sprawled down the length of the porch swing, his head resting near my shoulder. My arm lay along the back of the chair, behind him.

"It's funny that you say Tajikistan was your personal Waterloo," I said. "If I'd had to guess, I might have guessed Uganda. Your letters from Uganda were very … raw."

"Where do I begin?" one of his first letters from Uganda had started …

> *How can I relate northern Uganda to you when I feel often overwhelmed and confused by it myself?*
>
> *The war here is silent. No gunshots at night right now. Just occasional nights when the rebels abduct a few children to either conscript them as army/sex slaves or chop off their fingers/ears/lips and then release them back so as to promote as much fear as possible within the population.*
>
> *The villagers are terrified of the rebels. So they've migrated to centralized camps for "internally displaced peoples" (IDPs) where they can supposedly be protected by the government army. It's just, the war has been going on for 18 years now and the government doesn't seem to give a lick whether the rebels mutilate and kill the pesky northerners. And the government troops that are supposedly protecting people in the IDP camps sleep in the center of the camps, surrounded by the IDPs. Who's protecting who?*
>
> *The camps are awful. Masses of children with big eyes wearing tattered clothing, all with bulging bellies*

and flies buzzing around their faces. Idle men who used to farm fields sitting around getting drunk. Women walking long distances to collect water from dirty ponds using dirty plastic containers. Thatched mud and straw huts crammed so closely together that when the dry, dusty wind blows a cooking fire too far, the whole tinderbox camp goes up in flames. Piles of feces all over the ground. Desperate people begging me and expecting me to help them.

Mike fingered the stem of the wine glass he was holding as he thought about what I'd said about his Uganda emails. The drops of water beading the smooth surface of the glass reflected a dozen blue horizons. We watched them rotate as the glass turned. Nothing else stirred under the hot, heavy silence of that summer afternoon. We were an unfathomable distance from the desperation of those camps.

"Uganda was raw," Mike said. "But Tajikistan was harder. When I arrived in Tajikistan I thought I was extraordinary and indestructible. I thought that if I could live in solidarity with the poor and love Tajikistan and work hard enough, then the changes I wanted for that place and those people would happen and things would make sense. All of these expectations collided with a hard reality, and I was the one who broke." He shrugged. "By the time I got to Uganda… I don't know how you'd say it. I was less idealistic? I was less arrogant? I'd stopped expecting to feel as if I were saving the world every day. I'd accepted that humanitarian moments are rarer than you'd think in this work."

That was right, I remembered. He'd written about humanitarian moments in the second half of that letter from Uganda:

Sunday I was the ugly mzungo (foreigner). We work six days a week. I was looking forward to being able to sit on the veranda reading and sipping a cold glass of water that Sunday. I was looking forward to being able to eat lunch (we don't eat while we're in the camps because we just can't eat food in front of the people). I was looking forward to being able to forget, if only for a day, that on the other side of those iron gates are naked children with bloated bellies. But there's a cholera outbreak in Pabbo camp now, so Saturday night it was decided that we would work again on Sunday.

So Sunday I arrived at the office early. I figured the earlier we left the office, the earlier we could finish our work and the earlier I would be able to get home. There was just one hurdle in this plan: my staff. Rather than arrive early in the morning as we had agreed, they arrived late. And then, after leaving the office two hours behind schedule, we had to spend an additional half-hour getting some supplies they had forgotten.

The day in the camp was long, hot, frustrating, and as time went on I became more and more the ugly mzungo. You know, the foreigner who is short on patience and stressed out about everything.

Late in the day, after we had analyzed water from our last point, I was walking back from a spring. The spring is located about 10 minutes from the huts on the edge of the camp. It's a beautiful walk though lush banana trees, paddies bursting with amber rice shocks, rolling fields of cassava and sweet potatoes. Several women carrying yellow jerry cans to the spring passed us as we walked back to our truck. And just at that moment, right in the midst of all my ugliness

*that stemmed from the frustrating day at the end of a
wearisome week, just at that moment I realized that I
was catching a glimpse of something really beautiful: a
snapshot of what life must have been like for these people
before the start of the war 18 years ago. And hopefully a
snapshot of what life will be like for these people someday
when the war ends.*

*Until then I have the opportunity to serve these
people. Right now that means working to prevent the
cholera from spreading, in the hope that fewer of these
people die and can someday leave the camps and return
to their villages in the green rolling hills. And every now
and then I have a moment where my heart is filled with
love and compassion.*

*In humanitarian aid work, feel-good moments
are rarer than you might think. Most days are
painful struggle. Cross-cultural misunderstandings.
Being viewed as a wealthy vending machine. Feeling
perpetually compromised in your own beliefs, ideals, and
desires. Staring into the terrible face of intense suffering
knowing full well that you are completely unable to end
the suffering, that you barely even know where to begin.*

But, today, I had a humanitarian moment.

"I don't do it just for the humanitarian moments," Mike said.
"I don't think you *can* do this just for the humanitarian moments.
They're beautiful when they come, but they're not enough, and
there are not enough of them. I do my work now as best I can
because I still feel more passionate about this than anything else,
and I still believe it does more good than harm. What about you?
Why do you keep working to support humanitarian workers?
Why do you keep choosing this? The last essay I read before I

emailed you that first time was the one you wrote about alternate lives. I loved that essay."

Then he quoted my own writing to me: "Few of us who live in the Western world must do exactly what we do to feed and clothe ourselves. Many times our career choices are really more influenced by a cocktail of duty, fear, apathy, talent, priorities, and passion. Alternate lives, at least one or two of them, often lie within reach."

I stared out to sea again, through the haze hanging over the cane fields below us and into all that luxurious, promising space beyond.

"I don't have one good answer to this," I said. "I still often sit on planes wondering what I can possibly say in the workshops that I am going to give that would make it worth the time, the money, the energy and the risk to get there – for me and for them." Then I told him a story. "When we had to postpone the last set of Kenya workshops last year until October because of the violence, we ran some online discussion groups for counselors and humanitarian workers in Nairobi. One person, a child advocate, talked about how overwhelmed and powerless she felt. Stray bullets from the police had killed two of their students that week.

"We ended up talking a lot that session about that issue of feeling overwhelmed and powerless, and about what can anchor us in the midst of situations that provoke those feelings. What do we really have to offer as helpers, as counselors or humanitarian workers, when people are being killed on your neighborhood streets? What weapons do we really have to fight against feeling powerless?

"Someone in that session said that being there was critical, even if you didn't know what to say, that your mere presence was hope. They said that the fact that we were alive, and walking and talking and present, all sent a message that there was life and hope somewhere and that a different kind of future was possible. They said that we tend to focus only on the miracles that Jesus performed but that he must have spent most of his time simply walking among the people and that that, in itself, must have brought hope.

"This theme of the power of presence stuck with me. Presence can seem like such a small offering. I want to believe that sometimes when I show up I sow some seeds of hope in fields of violence and despair, but I'm not sure. When I stop to think about it, I am rarely completely sure of anything anymore."

I looked again at the dozen horizons glued to Mike's wine glass.

"I quoted Tolle in that alternate-lives essay," I said. "'Live every moment as if you had chosen it.' But perhaps I should also have quoted Rilke: 'Be patient toward all that is unsolved in your heart and try to love the questions themselves like locked rooms and like books that are written in a very foreign tongue. Do not now seek the answers, which cannot be given you because you would not be able to live them. And the point is, to live everything. Live the questions now. Perhaps you will then gradually, without noticing it, live along some distant day into the answer.'"

I cannot now remember what Mike said next, because as he said it he also reached up and slid his hand over mine, pulling my arm down around his shoulders and anchoring it against the living warmth of his chest.

I closed my eyes, blocking out the expanse of *there* for just a second, and felt his heartbeat against my palm.

ON DAY TEN MIKE sent out a mass email to his Melbourne

friends inviting them to come and meet his Aussie girlfriend during a drinks gathering down there in a couple of days. By this time I'd already figured out that Mike and I were on. That didn't stop me from teasing him about his presumption when the email landed in my inbox.

"We've talked about almost everything else under the sun but we couldn't manage to clarify our relationship status before addressing it in email?" I asked. "And not just any email, mind you, a mass email?"

Mike rolled his eyes and grinned.

"Technicality," he said.

By the time we parted ways five days later at Melbourne Airport, we were utterly exhausted, emotionally overloaded, and officially dating.

I sat alone in my departure lounge, waiting to board my flight back to Los Angeles, and thought about the charged intensity of the last two weeks – of Mike's smile, the way he made me laugh, the night we finally shared our first kiss and the sandy applause I heard when I dropped the pair of sandals I was holding to the beach so that I could wrap my arms around him. Then I wondered whether I would ever see Mike again.

Los Angeles – Accra – **Washington, D.C.** – Sydney – Zagreb – South Bend – Nairobi – San Diego – Atlanta – **Madang** – Kona – Canberra – London – Baltimore – Itonga – Vancouver – Harare – Dushanbe – Lira – Petats – Port Moresby – Brisbane – Ballina - Malibu

LOVE LONG DISTANCE

Los Angeles, USA

I NEVER DID GET an answer to the letter I sent to Travis telling him I'd be moving out a couple of days after I got back to L.A. I didn't get an answer to the letter I sent to his sister and mother either – a long, frank record of what I had seen unfold over the previous eight months. Without more tangible family support and some antipsychotic medication, I told them, I wasn't sure how much longer Travis could continue to cope the way he was currently coping. His life was unraveling.

When I boarded the plane in Melbourne, I wasn't sure what I'd find on the other end of my journey. It probably wasn't the wisest decision I've ever made to get off the plane in Los Angeles and go straight back to our apartment alone, but that's what I did.

I was hugely relieved when I got there to find Travis at home, alive, and in apparently decent spirits. As it turned out, he had gotten my letter and wasn't overjoyed that I was moving out, but he didn't appear to be unduly dented by the news either. He didn't mention anything about my letters to his family. And he was going to Las Vegas that weekend.

I was moved out by the time he got back.

More than a dozen of my friends showed up on Saturday to help me relocate. I am not used to being so completely on the receiving end of kindness, and it was profoundly overwhelming and touching to see this friendly troupe boxing up my kitchen, disassembling my bed, and carting my couch out the door. About five hours after we'd started I was standing alone in my new apartment, surrounded by hundreds of books piled in haphazard stacks, realizing that I hadn't contacted Edison about the electricity at the new apartment.

Hence I wouldn't have any for five days.

I didn't really mind not having any electricity. It was a good excuse not to do any unpacking after it got dark or buy groceries or cook for myself. At night I navigated by the light of my laptop screen while the computer battery lasted and pretended I was living in Botswana, until I remembered that I probably would not have a laptop if I really were living in Botswana. Then I pretended I was camping.

I HAD THOUGHT THAT I would mourn my old apartment. That place was layered with memories of hellos and goodbyes, movie nights and intimate dinners, long talks, laughter, and tears. I knew how to turn the tap just so for the right water temperature in the shower. I could walk downstairs at night in the dark to get a drink without fear of tripping. I knew the sound of the front door opening and closing, of the fountain that splashed in the courtyard. That familiarity was precious.

But by the time I finally moved out, none of that mattered in the slightest anymore. I still did feel sad and angry, but it wasn't over losing a place. On that front I felt nothing but relief and exhaustion. At some point since Travis had fallen through a portal in his mind, that apartment had ceased to be a home. The uncertainty, helplessness and fear I felt in the face of his unpredictable volatility had rendered familiarity completely moot and vanquished any sense of sanctuary. It had become more emotionally taxing to come home in the evenings than to travel solo to Nairobi.

My new apartment was devoid of electricity, gas, home phone, internet, and memories, but it was pure joy to leave work and be able to relax instead of having to take the energy levels up another notch. It was luxury to walk into space that was empty and silent. I loved that the walls in this new place were painted a cheerful panoply of yellow, orange and red. I loved seeing the mountains from the kitchen as they traced out a jagged horizon behind the tops of the palm trees. I loved the two big trees in the courtyard that formed a thick green shield against my neighbor's windows.

If the electricity company had told me that it couldn't turn the power on for a year, I would just have bought a flashlight and stayed anyway.

———— ◦∞◦ ————

I WASN'T THE ONLY one who left Australia and returned to a chaotic move on the home front. In the wake of the last robbery, Mike's colleagues had indeed moved him out in his absence. He returned to Papua New Guinea to find what remained of his belongings piled in boxes in his area manager's office.

"I can't look through it just yet," he wrote to me. "I can't bear to find out what's not there."

What Mike had instead of worldly possessions was a new boss, a new house and a new housemate, Tristan, who was out in the field the night Mike arrived but who'd thoughtfully left behind a set of keys and a note letting Mike know he'd killed seventy cockroaches in the new place the night before. Also, Mike had a new girlfriend on the other side of the world.

We were so used to communicating via letters that we hadn't give much thought to whether or how we were actually going to *talk* once we'd decided to date. And with both of us moving and returning to work, thieves having relieved Mike of his laptop microphone, and limited access to the internet on both sides of the Pacific, we also didn't figure out the talking thing until some time after we had returned to our respective sides of the world.

Two weeks after getting back to L.A. I was sitting on the couch in my new apartment on a Saturday night, writing, when my mobile phone rang. The display read "No Caller ID," which usually meant someone overseas, and I picked it up expecting my brother.

The line wasn't working that well and neither was my brain, apparently. Before I relay the conversation, I have to pause for some disclaimers. I didn't know that Mike had my mobile phone number. I wasn't sure it was technically possible for him to call me from where he was. I had never talked to him on the phone before. And I was writing. I was therefore vague. Very vague.

"Hi," Mike said. "So, do you like surprises?"

Hmmm, it's a guy's voice. Not Matt. Probably foreign friend. Possibly foreign friend flying into L.A. tonight who wants a couch to crash on. Crap, I don't want to drive to LAX to pick someone up tonight! "Uh ... sometimes."

Mike said something about sitting on a rock looking out over the Pacific Ocean.

Hmmm, mystery guy friend trying to mess with me by pretending to be Mike. Who would be that mean? Okay, let's face it, a lot of my friends would be that mean.

I had no idea who it was, but for some reason I was firmly convinced that it *wasn't* Mike. After we'd traded several more sentences I finally sighed and asked, "Ah, who is this?"

"Your secret admirer from PNG."

Hmmmm, he didn't say Mike, *he said* secret admirer. *That's something a mean friend might say.*

It took about three awkward minutes for me to accept that it actually *was* Mike, and about thirty seconds after that (while I was still trying to pretend that I normally acted like such a weirdo at the start of phone calls) the line went dead. I was left with no way to call him back and no way to even debrief by sending an email, because the new apartment didn't yet have working internet. I went to bed with the phone that night in case Mike managed to ring again and stewed for hours about the fact that I hadn't recognized my own boyfriend's voice on the phone and must have come across as a suspicious freak.

Were we insane to think we could make this work? I mean, how often do you really hear of long-distance relationship success stories outside of novels set before or during World War II?

AFTER ALL THE TIME we spent in Australia sitting on my parents' porch swing and talking about every topic under the sun (a time Mike referred to with a straight face and complete seriousness as our "due diligence period"), we entered the long-distance dating game confident. I even told Mike, one warm afternoon, that I was good at distance.

Mike, I found out later, had thought that was particularly amusing.

"Hello, Lisa who's good at distance," Mike emailed me a couple of days after our Melbourne farewells, in response to a note of my own bemoaning our separation. "This is Mike who's not good at remembering details, but he remembered that particular detail because he wanted to tell Lisa that she was on crack but figured that might ruin the moment on the porch swing, and Lisa might think he was an insensitive ape, and then Lisa would kick his ass onto the first plane to Melbourne and Mike wasn't prepared for that. But now that some time has passed and approximately 7,000 miles of ocean buffer us: You are *so* on crack."

"I would like to point out," I wrote back, "that however hard this first week apart has felt, we must both be somewhat good at distance or we would never have decided to embark on this crazy path. Being good at it, however, doesn't mean it doesn't still suck. I am quite talented at doing a number of things I really hate."

Whether or not Mike and I really *were* good at distance, distance was probably good for us in some important ways.

Having nothing to build our relationship with but words for the following three months forced us to cover a lot of ground. Doing this when we couldn't exchange text messages and were only able to talk by Skype every couple of days for an hour or two also removed some of the pressures and pitfalls that attend 24-hour accessibility and the possibility of instantaneous response. Distance slowed us down, granted us extra time and space to think, and encouraged us to be deliberate and thorough in our communication.

But the distance was also often difficult. There was the temptation to feel as if my "real life" was on hold until Mike arrived in May for a month of holidays – to live in such a haze of anticipation that it obscured the beauty of the present. It took effort and energy to rearrange my schedule so that we could talk, or to prioritize writing letters when I was exhausted or flat. Mike was sometimes out in the villages and beyond even the reach of cell phones for a week or more, and these stretches of silence sometimes assaulted my sense of surety in the concept of us and prompted mood swings that hit without warning. I could be grocery shopping, looking forward to a quiet night at home with Indian food, red wine and my laptop, and then glance up to see a couple ahead of me, hand in hand, and I'd be swamped by a sudden wave of longing or doubt.

In those moments I never had the option of reaching for the phone just so I could hear Mike's voice, and even when we *were* talking during our carefully scheduled Skype dates, it wasn't guaranteed to be smooth and happy sailing. Occasionally we'd be chattering away easily one minute only to find ourselves mired in a messy miscommunication the next. Or we'd be laughing and a moment later one of us would have blundered unexpectedly into a virtual minefield.

This was the situation we found ourselves in late one night, about a month before Mike was to arrive in L.A. for his May holiday. We'd been talking for an hour already, but before we wrapped up I suggested we dip into the question box.

The question box was a game we used sometimes to help move us past the whats, whens, and hows of our days. A solid plastic rectangle, it held hundreds of small cards each printed with a different question.

What is one special holiday memory from childhood?

If you had to move to a foreign country indefinitely, which one would you choose?

What's your favorite flavor of ice cream?

This night, however, the card that I randomly selected focused on a topic much weightier than ice cream. I took a glance and wondered whether I should throw it back and pick another one.

"What's the question?" Mike asked after I'd been silent for a couple of seconds.

"Okay," I said, deciding to stick with it, "what's the most important quality in a marriage?"

"Commitment," Mike said immediately. Then he paused and talked around this concept for a while, trying on words like *honesty* and *forgiveness*.

"No," he finally said decisively. "Commitment."

Sleepy and relaxed, I opened my mouth and started to think out loud. "I don't think so," I said. "I think it's affection or warmth or … kindness. Yeah, kindness. I'd rank that above commitment."

There was silence on the other end of the Skype line.

"Hello?" I said.

"Is that because commitment would already be there?" Mike asked.

"I guess so," I said. "I can't easily see a relationship that's full of affection and kindness not being built on some foundation of commitment, but I *can* envision it the other way around – a committed relationship lacking kindness – and that's just ugly."

Again, silence.

"Hello?" I said.

"I'm a bit paralyzed right now," the distant Mike finally replied. "I think I'm better at commitment than I am at affection. I don't think I can discuss this anymore at the moment. I have to get back to the office over here anyway."

"Oh," I said, startled. "Uh, okay. That's not one of my fears in relation to us by the way, that you're not good at affection, but all right."

"It's not you, I've just stumbled over some of my own inner furniture," Mike managed to reassure me before signing off. "We'll talk soon."

We did talk soon, but not before I spent an uncomfortable couple of days wondering where I'd gone wrong. Perhaps, I ventured to my parents after thinking it through, it was the moment when I opened my mouth after Mike had bared his soul and insinuated that I didn't think commitment was that big a deal and that I'd be in a marriage only as long as the other person was being kind.

"Yeah, that might have done it, I'd say," Mum said.

"Mum!" I said.

"I'm sure it'll be fine," she said, negating any reassurance the statement might have delivered by laughing immediately afterward.

"I *do* think commitment is hugely important," I said. "And I know any commitment – to marriage, to a place – is going to have times when it's tested. I was just saying that I'm not sure commitment is the be-all and the end-all. I mean, would I really want to stay in a marriage indefinitely if commitment was all it had going for it? Commitment might be effective glue, but surely kindness or something else *has* to be present much of the time to make it worth holding something together?"

Mum didn't venture to touch that one.

"What do *you* think is the most important quality in a marriage, then?" I asked her.

"Balance," she said.

"Balance?" asked my father, who'd been listening in from the other side of the study.

"Balance," my mother repeated firmly. "What have other people said?"

"Well, two of my colleagues said trust," I said, "and another one said goodwill. They defined that as the commitment to hold a good image of that person in your mind even when you're not liking them in the moment."

"Does anyone want to know what I think?" Dad asked in my favorite tone of voice, that of the patient martyr.

Apparently it's Mum's favorite tone of voice, too, because she was quicker off the mark than I was.

"Not really," Mum said breezily.

"Yes, Dad," I said, rolling my eyes at both of them. "We want to know what you think."

"A commitment to love," he announced. "It combines commitment and kindness."

"That is not a single quality," Mum replied.

"And balance is?" Dad asked.

In one way, this opportunity Mike and I had to probe our joys, sorrows, and thoughts across the miles when we might otherwise have been discovering what snacks we each liked at the movie theater was providing us with a deep and solid foundation. But it was also rendering our quirks as adorable abstractions and robbing us of small daily opportunities to identify differences and head off or resolve conflict. Then, when we did happen to stumble into these differences or miscommunications, they often seemed magnified by the miles between us. I had made huge progress since the end of my relationship with Jason, and I no longer shied away at the first hint of potential conflict. I still didn't *enjoy* conflict, however, and although Mike (despite his fears on this front) was excellent at communicating affection across the miles, we couldn't always resolve a conversation satisfactorily when one of us stumbled across our inner furniture. During those times, I had to battle to control my own insecurities and learn to live with the tension of the unresolved until we could talk things out.

There were more than a handful of days when one or both of us struggled to stay grounded.

"Since leaving the office yesterday afternoon, I've felt blah," Mike wrote to me a couple of weeks after we parted ways in Melbourne. "No one particular reason, and that makes it more difficult. I don't like feeling blah; it means that I don't feel like doing anything, that I don't feel excited about anything. It means absence of passion. I fear blah. So how about to our official post-Ballina discussion topics list I add: 'What do you do when you feel blah?'"

"When I feel blah everything sort of flattens out and goes two-dimensional," I replied. "The day elongates and everything takes more effort – doing the 'shoulds' of the day, talking to people, caring. I don't taste fun. It's like the bubbles go out of life. On the worst days, nothing I say or do comes out quite right and I feel as if I'm talking to people through an invisible filter that's skewing everything, the way that gazing at objects underwater distorts perception. And what do I do when I feel like this? That's a question I wish I had a simple answer to."

———————

ONE OF THE WAYS I fought the blah that often threatened during those three months of separation was working to create a home out of the new apartment.

I'd arrived in L.A. more than four years earlier with only two suitcases and I'd resisted buying anything that felt too big and too permanent for a very long time. Anything I really did need – a bed, for example – I bought secondhand from online marketplace forums.

But this move, I was determined, would be different.

I would commit to this new beginning by transforming the

blank slate of the new apartment into a haven of tranquility, I resolved. I imagined dark wood, white bedding, clean lines, and minimal clutter, a space in which creativity would flourish like grape vines in France, somewhere you would breathe more deeply and slowly the minute you entered. I wanted a wooden counter-height kitchen table with six tall chairs. I wanted a bright Moroccan-tiled console in the entry. I wanted brand-new sophisticated blue couches and low coffee tables. I wanted stuff to match. And I was determined that I was going to buy it new, like a normal person. I was *not* going to impulse-buy off secondhand forums and risk ending up with a couch covered in dog hair or a bread-maker that I would never use. This time I was going to plan ahead and make sensible choices. Choices I'd thought through carefully.

It took less than two weeks after the move, however, for me to discover a couple of flaws in that grand plan.

First, money. Who knew that new stuff cost *so much money???* Even the cheapest decent counter-height dining-room table would set me back close to a thousand dollars. Second, the time and energy it takes to think through such choices carefully. After a couple of days spent cruising furniture stores online and walking around them in my new neighborhood, I was done with the whole process. I didn't, I learned, really want to spend days thinking about dining-room tables. And all the furniture in these stores was a shiny sort of bland.

So it was that less than a month after moving I found myself back on the online forums hawking secondhand goods, and on my first virtual peregrination I saw it.

A television cabinet made out of dark teak wood. Perched on four solid legs, it stood more than six feet tall and two feet deep. The doors were delicately arched, fronted with slender bars, and double-hinged so that they unfolded to swing all the way back. It cost a hundred and thirty dollars.

It was probably a little strange that in an apartment devoid of kitchen table, microwave, and lamps, my first major purchase would be a huge cabinet for a TV I didn't own and was not at all sure that I wanted to acquire. But the second I saw those dark wooden curves I *knew* that exciting creative adventures would unfold for the person who owned this piece of furniture, that it would infuse my new living room with mystery and potential, that the cabinet *wanted* me to buy it. So on Saturday I drove down to Hollywood to seal the deal.

On the way home I started to think about how I was going to pick up the cabinet later that week as promised, and the next day I emailed my friend Nick and asked if he'd like me to take him out to dinner on Thursday, via Hollywood, in his truck.

As my preferred partner in crime for adventures related to sourcing secondhand furniture, this was not the first time Nick had received such an invitation from me. Nick was blessed with the spiritual gift of "large vehicle." Nick also seemed willing to view these occasional forays less as "running all over town on Lisa's errands" than as "quality friendship time on the freeways with intermittent heavy lifting to keep things interesting."

That Thursday Nick turned up and asked pertinent questions before we even set out. It seemed he had learned a couple of things over the years from these outings (although not, apparently, that perhaps the wisest course of action was just to say no and not set out at all).

"How big is this thing again?" Nick asked.

I told him. And I was honest.

"And once we get it back here, how are we going to get it from the curb, three hundred feet down winding sidewalks and up two flights of stairs into your apartment?" he asked.

I confessed that this was a question I had thought about

myself several times during the previous four days but that I had not yet managed to come up with a good answer.

"I'm not particularly proud of that," I finished lamely. "It's not something I'd normally do – ask you to help me when I'm not sure how it's not going to kill the two of us to try to move this thing."

"Are you kidding?" Nick said. "That totally sounds like something you'd normally do to me."

"I'm sure something will work out," I said, shooting for optimism more out of desperation than any real conviction that I was right.

Down in Hollywood it took Nick and me, the seller, and two hapless bystanders to get the cabinet into the back of Nick's truck, and by the time we got back to my place at a quarter past ten that night I still hadn't figured out a grand relocation plan. As we pulled up in front of my apartment complex, it was quiet and dark. There were no able-bodied stranger-neighbors roaming around whom I could beg to help us, but I did find a dolly sitting conveniently outside someone's door waiting to be borrowed, and after fifteen minutes of extreme exertion Nick had managed to wrestle the cabinet to the bottom of the stairs.

Then we were stuck.

Nick eventually asked the obvious. "How are we going to get it up there?"

"If we just *look* at it for a while we'll figure something out," I said.

Ten minutes later we were still looking at it. And we still had not figured anything out.

"That's the biggest TV cabinet I've ever seen," Nick said. "It looks like the wardrobe in the C.S. Lewis movies. You know, the entrance to Narnia?"

"It does!" I agreed, amazed.

"Perhaps if we climb inside it will *fly* up the stairs?" Nick said sarcastically.

"You know," he added in a tone laced with frustration, affection, and bewilderment, "I never really understood the whole concept of love/hate until I met you."

As I was laughing at this, a muscled neighbor named Tony whom I had met only five hours earlier, an angel sipping Starbucks, walked up from the garage and said those holy words: "Looks like you need some help."

"Even with Tony's help," I wrote to Mike later that night, "it took us another ten minutes and several near-hernias to get the cabinet up the stairs and through my door, but it was totally worth it. Who needs predictable new furniture when you can have furniture with a back story? Who even needs a TV inside a cabinet that already hints at whole other worlds removed from the mundane in this one – worlds of snow and crocuses, danger and sacrifice, adventure and valor? No, I'm convinced that this cabinet will make me a better writer, indeed a better person. It is, after all, a gateway to Narnia. And you can never have too many of those in your life."

———⨏⨏⨏———

AFTER I ACQUIRED NARNIA, other bits and pieces of furniture fell into place. Over the next couple of months, I granted a home to dozens of books in two enormous Spanish-style wooden bookshelves. I flanked my bed with nightstands that housed gentle lamps. I hung pictures of peaceful beaches in Australia and wistful children in Belize. I found a secondhand kitchen table, and friends gave me a coffee table. I bought delicate, sensual wine glasses. I found the perfect nooks for a bronze statue from Ghana, ebony candlesticks from Kenya, and a bowl from Indonesia made entirely of cinnamon. Out on the deck I planted forget-me-nots in a small pot and watered them faithfully until they, much to my amazed excitement, pushed up fragile green shoots.

Then I forgot to water them for more than a week and they died, but never mind. The important point was that I was finally putting energy into creating my own homey space. It didn't end up looking much like the home I'd initially envisioned – nothing was dark wood except the Narnia cabinet, you couldn't say that things *matched* exactly, and it was all far more comfortably cheerful than uncluttered elegance – but with all these different woods and shapes and colors cobbled together, it worked. It felt like a visual of my life. It felt just right.

Being so far from Mike, on the other hand, didn't feel just right. There were many moments from February to May when I wished rather acutely that we lived in the same city instead of being separated by the Pacific Ocean and an 18-hour time difference.

Near Madang, PNG

ON FEBRUARY 14TH MIKE was out in the field and totally out of contact. As he put it later, he was "celebrating Valentine's Day in true PNG style, by sleeping in a village surrounded by other men's wives."

"One thing we're not going to have to worry about this year," I wrote in response to this, "is setting any expectations too high for future celebration of events like Valentine's Day or birthdays."

Washington, D.C., USA

THREE WEEKS LATER, ON Mike's birthday, I was in Washington, D.C., again for work. Perhaps, Mike had suggested, while I was there I might like to meet his parents, who lived nearby? I thought this over and then shrugged and agreed. After all, I reasoned, Mike had braved my parents' house within two hours of meeting me; I could brave his alone. So on a cold spring night, I borrowed Michelle's car, bought a bunch of flowers, and showed up for dinner at Mike's parents' house.

Mike's parents were utterly hospitable, if seemingly a little puzzled by my presence on the scene.

"So," his mother ventured shortly after I arrived, while I was still processing the framed high school portrait of Mike that was sitting in the living room, "how did you two first meet? Was it in Thailand?"

I tore my eyes away from a smiling eighteen-year-old Mike with some difficulty.

What? Sure, Mike hasn't seen them since we met, but hasn't he told them the whole story?

"Not exactly," I said. "Here's how it happened …"

After my own mother's chicken-dance antics in the kitchen on the night that Mike arrived in Australia, I was gleeful to have plenty to report back to Mike by email after dinner.

"Your parents were utterly hospitable," I started my letter. "A turkey had been roasted, rolls baked, profiteroles procured and fruit salad made. And your mother will no doubt tell you she did not show me the baby albums. That is true. She thoughtfully left them on the coffee table and I looked through them all by myself while dinner was being put on the table.

"I can also report the following:

"1. You have quite a considerable pile of stuff stored in that house. I *think* it is still less than what I have stored in my parents' house, but even after looking it over carefully during the parent-guided tour of the basement, I'm not sure.

"2. Your mother made me pose for photographs before I left because she said she would be in terrible trouble with the other women at the office if she went in on Monday morning without pictures.

"3. Within half an hour of meeting me your mother asked whether we were going to have an e-marriage. In her defense the flow of the conversation went like this: I explained how we met and ended with, 'so now we're e-dating.' Your Mum said, 'E-dating. What comes next, an e-marriage and e-kids?'"

Los Angeles, USA

THREE WEEKS LATER, ON *my* birthday, Mike was out in the field again. But I did have a birthday present to open that morning when I woke up.

He had sent me a *billum* (a woven bag used by villagers in PNG to carry everything from vegetables to babies) and a CD full of photographs. This wasn't just any *billum*. Mike had clearly gone to some trouble to find the most outrageously bright red, pink and orange *billum* in existence. Then he'd carried this *billum* with him everywhere for several weeks, taking pictures along the way to demonstrate everything I could do with this most useful of gifts.

The *billum* had sat beside Mike on the porch of his house. It had been slung over his shoulder while he went jogging, snorkeling, swimming, scuba diving, and did sunrise yoga. The *billum* had accompanied Mike to the office, the markets, and on Skype dates. The *billum* had even taken showers under the drain spout. The last photo on the disk showed Mike, the *billum*, and a handwritten happy-birthday sign with a big red heart on it.

I laughed at these seventy-five photos until I almost cried.

Then I read his card and, again, almost cried.

"Do you think these feelings are going to continue?" it started. "I never thought it would happen to me. I was always a bit skeptical about becoming paralyzed by love. No, that couldn't happen to me. And now it has. ...

"I still feel a bit uneasy about this. I never expected it and now it's here," he finished, a page and a half later. "Not skeptical anymore. But perhaps scared of what will happen. Will these feeling last? Will we make it?"

Los Angeles – Accra – Washington, D.C. – Sydney – Zagreb – South Bend – Nairobi – San Diego – Atlanta – Madang – Kona – Canberra – London – Baltimore – Itonga – Vancouver – Harare – Dushanbe – Lira – Petats – Port Moresby – Brisbane – Ballina – **Malibu**

Shock and Awe in Love

I'D ALWAYS WONDERED HOW someone is caught by surprise by a marriage proposal in this day and age. I mean, if you're in a solid relationship and you're both good communicators, surely you'd have some idea if one party in that equation were scheming to pop the question? I mean, how dumb *are* people?

So, yeah, apparently I'm dumb.

Well, that's one possibility. Another possibility is that Mike is crazy. Or Mike could be both dumb and crazy. Or I could be. Or maybe we both are.

Even now I'm still undecided on this point, but let me back up and set the scene, because setting the scene is a valuable life skill that should be exercised during the telling of all stories (and quite possibly, I've come to believe, in advance of all major life-altering decisions).

Los Angeles, USA

BY APRIL, THREE MONTHS after first meeting in Australia, Mike and I had made our first tentative forays toward discussing when Mike was going to leave Papua New Guinea and move to L.A.

His contract in PNG wasn't up until December, and I didn't let myself spend much time considering the possibility that he might cut it short. I knew what I was getting into when I signed on to this relationship, I told myself. I was determined not to be *that* woman – the one who expects her man to rearrange all his plans and priorities around her preferences.

No, we hadn't exactly discussed it yet, but I had it all worked out in my head. Mike was going to stay in PNG until December, as he'd planned. We would soldier through this year of long-distance dating, spending a month together in the U.S. in May and two weeks in September in Cambodia. We'd meet again in Australia for Christmas and then Mike would move to L.A. in January. With all continuing to go well, we'd date for four to six months while living in the same city and then (and here was another topic I wasn't letting myself think too much about) we would get engaged.

It was such a *good* plan. Such a *sensible* plan.

I just assumed that it was also Mike's plan.

So I was very surprised when, in April, Mike dropped the first hints that he might consider leaving PNG in September rather than December.

It was raining in Madang that day. When it rained we couldn't talk, because the internet connection had slowed way down. We could usually, however, instant-message. So that's what we were doing when Mike, mid-conversation, joked about quitting his job.

After I read this comment I didn't send any words back straight away. I just used the party emoticon, the one where a little yellow face, crowned with a purple hat, is tooting a paper horn and streamers are floating down. Instant-message conversations are not entirely devoid of nonverbal signals if you make full use of the emoticons.

Mike laughed. This I know because he wrote "LOL" (laugh out loud). Twice.

"Not fair," he wrote. "You weren't supposed to have that reaction."

"Look," I wrote, "just because I fully support you staying in PNG for the year doesn't mean I wouldn't throw a party if you decided not to."

"So what about perseverance?" Mike teased.

"Stuff perseverance," I shot back. "It's like a vaccine. Once you've had a dose or two you're good for ten years."

"Fifteen," Mike wrote. "Twenty. Life."

"Exactly," I said.

"I wish," Mike said.

I sent a smiley face.

"We were talking about this over here last night," Mike said. "The consensus was that perseverance is worth it if there's some sort of future goal you want to achieve."

"What qualifies as a worthwhile goal?" I said.

"I threw that one out there, but no responses," Mike said, "and you don't expect me to have my own original answer now, do you?"

"Oh, no, sorry. That *is* asking a bit much," I said. "But I just think you can set up anything as a goal, but some goals are not going to be worth it."

"A worthwhile goal isn't just 'I made a commitment and I'll be damned if I renege even if it *kills* me'??" Mike replied.

"I don't think so." I said. "That's just being unable to reroute despite changing circumstances. I don't think that alone is a good enough goal in most situations."

"What about if the joy in the situation is gone. Then perseverance isn't worthwhile?" Mike typed.

"Joy gone for how long?" I asked. "It's such a tricky one. I think we have times when the joy *is* gone but we're still supposed to stick it out. Other times joy going is a huge red warning flag."

"No formula on this," Mike said.

"Yeah," I said. "No formula. Guess that's what we're supposed to need wisdom for."

"The other tidbit of wisdom that came to me last night ..." Mike said.

"Yeah?"

"No need to make a decision about PNG until the end of May," Mike said. "So how about that? We enjoy hanging out in May, and then the last week of May we make a decision. Okay?"

"Uh, I'm a little behind here," I sent back after a brief pause. "So you really *are* thinking seriously about not staying until December?"

This time Mike used the party emoticon.

"Yeah," he said.

"I didn't think it was in the *serious* zone yet," I said. "I thought it was in the *thinking* zone. Huh. Good to know."

"Thinking → serious can happen quite quickly for me," Mike wrote.

Malibu, USA

I THOUGHT THAT OUR not talking about Mike leaving PNG until the end of May was wise. It meant we could have a relaxed month. A month that as much as possible simulated a normal relationship. A month full of talking and all those aspects of dating that are pretty hard to replicate over Skype, no matter how creative you are with emoticons. A month to see whether we really *were* as good together face-to-face as we were over distance. I was really looking forward to sharing candlelight dinners, movies, picnic blankets, strawberries, glasses of wine, touch. And a week after Mike arrived in L.A., that's exactly what we were doing.

No, not touching. A picnic blanket, a grassy quiet hill, my favorite white wine, macadamia nuts, cheese and crackers, sunset, and the Pacific Ocean.

"Ah, Australia," we said, looking out to sea as we toasted the Pacific.

"It's just over there," I said fondly, pointing.

"Well," Mike said diplomatically, "you *could* get to Australia that way … if you wanted to go through Ecuador first."

He handed me a strawberry.

"So," he teased. "We have this whole list of topics to talk about that we haven't tackled over Skype. What weighty topic do you want to discuss tonight?"

Tired after the emotional intensity of our first week together and all the talking we'd already done, I took the easy way out.

"You pick," I said, smiling magnanimously.

"I don't want to talk about anything on the list tonight," Mike said

"Oh, okay," I said, thinking that Mike must *finally* have had his fill of intensity and was after light and fluffy banter. "Pick something else then, any topic."

"Any topic? Any topic it all? Do you realize the power you've given me?"

"Use it wisely," I said, lazily wondering where he was going to go with it.

—— ∞∞∞ ——

WHICH WAS WHEN HE got on his knees in front of me and said, "Lisa Marie McKay, will you marry me?"

—— ∞∞∞ ——

BEFORE TOTAL SHOCK SET in three seconds later I thought, "WHAT???? Lisa, focus! You've just been asked a yes-or-no question. The answer is absolutely, categorically not no. So, uh, it must be… yes?"

So that is what I said. Or probably more accurately, that is what I squeaked.

—— ∞∞∞ ——

THE REST OF THE evening is a bit jumbled in my mind, less a blur than a slide show. I remember certain things very clearly and others not at all.

Right after I said yes, Mike pulled out not one engagement ring but eight.

"You would not *believe* how hard it is to research diamonds over a dial-up internet connection," Mike said, waving a long string of woven cane rings around and talking very fast. "I've been trying to figure this out for *weeks*. I was completely sure I needed to have a ring until my colleague Sue told me, 'Question first, ring later.' So I figured a cane ring would be a good start. Plus, this way you can just pick the one that fits."

"Okay," I said, sliding one cane ring after another onto my finger.

"That one," I said, pointing to a small one near the end of the chain.

Mike cut it free from its neighbors with his pocketknife and slid it onto my finger.

"So, where do you want to get married?" Mike asked.

I looked at him blankly. Who was Sue? Where did I want to get married? What had just happened?

"Weeks?" I said. "You've been thinking about this for *weeks*? Let's start at the beginning."

"Okay," he said, "but we've got to meet your parents at the restaurant at seven."

"My parents know?"

"I emailed them ten days ago," Mike said.

THE BEACHSIDE MALIBU RESTAURANT we went to that night was gorgeous and the food was incredible. I took the fact that I was actually able to eat as a good sign (although worryingly, and completely out of character for me, I wasn't able to finish dessert).

As Mike and my parents filled me in on the back story, I became progressively more overwhelmed. Mike's weeks of planning and data-gathering about rings and proposal venues. How he had emailed my parents from PNG telling them what he was planning and asking if they could spend the day together after Mum and Dad arrived in L.A. five days after he did. How the three of them had talked all morning on Friday while I was at work getting mock-kidnapped by drunken militia during a security training exercise.

"I wanted to organize it so your parents would be the first people we'd see after the proposal," Mike said. "So it worked out perfectly that they were here in L.A. this weekend on their way to Washington."

"What did you talk about on Friday?" I asked.

"I asked for their blessing and their concerns," Mike said. "It was all very natural, comfortable. It was great."

"We asked whether you were expecting this," Mum said.

"I asked whether he thought you'd say yes," Dad said.

That counted as "comfortable" and "great"? I sneaked a look at Mike. He seemed unfazed.

"I said absolutely," Mike said. "On both counts."

"I said I wasn't so sure," Dad said.

Then, it seemed, they had started to talk odds.

"I thought there was a 95 percent chance of yes," Mike said, "a 4 percent chance of 'wait,' and less than 1 percent chance of no."

"I said I wasn't so sure," Dad said.

I didn't ask Dad what his guesses had been.

I also didn't say that I'd totally forgotten that "wait" might be a viable answer.

"The way I saw it," Mike said, "'yes' or 'wait' were both wins anyway. I just wanted you to know exactly where I stand and that I want to commit to spending the rest of my life with you. So it was win-win, really." Not for the first time, I admired Mike's capacity for dauntless optimism. "Then your parents spent the rest of the morning telling me that my plan to surprise you at sunset over a glass of wine in Malibu wasn't credible enough and we needed to tweak it to come up with something that was absolutely airtight. I really didn't want you to figure it out and ruin the story, because I know you need stories."

I bit my lip.

"Mike," I said. "You just proposed to me after we've spent three weeks, total, in the same country. I don't think story was ever going to be our biggest problem."

Los Angeles, USA

After dinner, after we'd driven back to L.A., and after we'd dropped my parents off at their motel, Mike and I talked until almost 2 a.m.

It was then that a somewhat sobered Mike began to realize how far off our respective timelines had been.

"I thought we weren't going to talk about your leaving the field until the end of the month," I said to him.

"Yeah," Mike said, looking puzzled. "I wanted you to have the security of knowing my intentions before we talked about that. Me leaving PNG and moving to L.A. has a big impact on your life."

"Not as big as us getting *married*!" I said. "I would have been fine with you moving to L.A. without us being engaged."

"Huh," Mike said. "I guess I misjudged that one. I half feel like I should apologize, but I'm not sure what for, because *I'm happy* we're engaged."

He grinned despite his abashment, and I laughed.

"I need some time," I said, stumbling over my explanation, not even quite sure what I was trying to say. "I want to give this decision some room to breathe. I need some time to process and focus on us rather than having all my energy go to dealing with the deluge of questions that *will* come when we tell people, you know."

The answer, I told Mike that night, was both yes and wait. I didn't know whether that meant waiting for two days, two weeks, or two years. But one thing I did know in the midst of this out-of-body-experience was that I didn't want to start on a long list of "people to tell" and risk repeated conversations along the lines of:

Lisa: Mike and I are engaged.

Good friend No. 23 (looking totally stunned): Oh my *word*! Isn't that a bit fast?

Lisa: Uh, yeah, I'm a bit thrown by it myself. I didn't think we'd be addressing this question *quite* yet.

Good friend No. 23 (delicately): Are you sure you know what you doing?

Lisa (edging toward hysteria): I think so. I really think I do. All my instincts say yes. But then I came home this afternoon and he was cleaning my kitchen and playing Shakira and I realized that I didn't know he likes Shakira, and I don't know what music is on his iPod, and is it safe to agree to marry someone when you don't know what music is on their iPod? Is it?? Huh??? HUH????"

Good friend No. 23: Um …

So at 2 a.m. after a rather exhausting conversation – the kind of conversation that anyone would want to have on the night she gets engaged, really – I said yes to something else that Mike offered me that night and did something I'd never done before.

I took Valium.

THE NEXT MORNING I dropped Mike off at my place after church on Sunday and went out for coffee with my parents.

"Take your time," Dad said anxiously. "Don't worry about how Mike's doing. He's had time to think this through. You just have to focus on whether or not this is what *you* want. Take as much time as you need."

"Oh," Mum said with a casual wave of one hand, "so he surprised you. So it's not exactly unfolding the way you thought it would. So you hit an unanticipated speed bump. You'll work it out. I think he's terrific." She grinned. "You know, there will be lots of good stories if you marry him."

"Merrilyn! *Please!*" my father said, agonized, both hands going to his forehead. "You do *not* marry someone because they'll give you *stories*."

"Oh I don't know," Mum said. "There are worse reasons."

"Don't worry," I said quickly, worried that Dad was courting a heart attack. "I'll take the time I need."

That turned out not to be two years, two months, or even two weeks. By Tuesday night I'd watched Mike hang on to a cheerful self-possession during three days of limbo and gone over and over it in my mind.

I wasn't absolutely sure that it was the right decision, frankly, but I also knew that I'm never one hundred percent sure about anything in life. It's just not in my nature. So just how sure did I need to be to make a commitment of this magnitude? Was it enough that I was a good sight surer of this than I'd been of any other major decision I'd ever made?

I WALKED INTO MY place Tuesday night to see my favorite flowers in a vase and some of Mike's favorites, red wine and dark chocolate, laid out on the coffee table.

"You got your favorite wine and chocolate the first time," Mike told me later. "It was my turn."

So it was that Mike, having judged that I was shaking off the shock, got down on one knee, again. And proposed, again.

"Because I wanted you to be able to remember it clearly," he said.

And so it was that I said yes. Again.

Upon Hearing the News

EILEEN SPENCER (LISA'S GRANDMOTHER, by phone)

Lisa: Nanna, I just wanted to let you know that Mike and I are engaged.

Nanna: (relief evident) Oh, good. We've waited and prayed for a *long* time for this! A *very* long time.

Lisa: NANNA!

Mike: (laughing) I've waited a long time for this, too, Nanna.

ROSEMARY WOLFE (MIKE'S MOTHER, by phone)

Mike: Lisa and I are engaged.

Rosemary: Does this mean I have to go somewhere for a wedding? People at the office suggested that since you've dated over email, perhaps you'd have an e-wedding and we could just log in?

MATT MCKAY (LISA'S BROTHER, by Skype)

Lisa: Mike and I are engaged.

Matt: Wow. Wow. Uh, *wow.* (Long pause) That's exciting. Wow. (Long pause) *He's* a man of action, that one. Wow.

252 | LISA MCKAY

(By Skype 24 hours later)

Matt: I think an engagement for longer than a couple of months might be good. Don't go to Vegas in the next three weeks, okay?

Lisa: I promise not to go to Vegas without telling you first.

TRAVIS (LISA'S FORMER FLATMATE, by phone)

Travis: Congratulations. (Pause) Are you serious? (After confirmation) Holy cow, you're the craziest person I know.

JUANITA GREY (LISA'S COUSIN, by phone)

Lisa: I thought I would ring and tell you I'm engaged.

Juanita: Oh, wow! I won't insult you by asking who to.

KATY VOSSWINKEL (MIKE'S FRIEND, by email)

"CONGRATULATIONS!!! You know, I don't think any engagement goes off the way you really think it's going to. Well some do, but they're cheesy."

TERESA MURRAY (MIKE'S FRIEND, by email)

"Congratulations! So happy for you and, see, you did find your mate while in the middle of nowhere. Thank God for technology. And you are not crazy, you just know what you want. Life is too short for waiting. I always knew it would be a woman who would get you out of the field."

BRANDON GOLM (MIKE'S COLLEGE ROOMMATE, by email)

"If she agrees to go to Vegas and get married now, I'll pay for one for your flights (offer valid in the continental U.S. only!)."

JOHANNA BRADLEY (LISA'S FRIEND, by email)

"Fantastic news!! I don't think this is too fast. Far too many people spend far too long thinking about getting married and miss a good year or two of marriage because they can't make a decision."

TASH WHITE (LISA'S FRIEND, by phone)

"That's great! Great!! I was pretty sure this was in the cards for you two."

DAVE SWEETING (MIKE'S FRIEND, by email)

"I was sweating a little halfway through your email. I thought Lisa was going to change her mind. But a happy ending after all, phew. So I'm guessing, at this rate, liklik pikininis (little children) by Christmas!?"

DAVE BAKER (MIKE'S FRIEND, by email)

"So, which God-forsaken, disease-ridden, Kalashnikov-toting, despair-inducing, horsehair-jock self-flagellating, barren/jungle/windswept wasteland will the wedding be in?"

Los Angeles – Accra – Washington, D.C. – Sydney – Zagreb – South Bend – Nairobi – San Diego – Atlanta – Madang – Kona – Canberra – London – Baltimore – Itonga – Vancouver – Harare – Dushanbe – Lira – Petats – Port Moresby – Brisbane – **Ballina** – Malibu

THE DAY BEFORE

"Every day is a journey, and the journey itself is home."
(Basho)

Ballina, Australia

WE DECIDED NOT TO go for disease-ridden, Kalashnikov-toting, or despair-inducing when it came to picking a wedding venue. We decided to go home.

Mine, to be precise.

Or my parents', to be more precise.

It's been eight months since Mike proposed and four months since he packed up in Papua New Guinea and moved his life to Los Angeles. We did toy with the idea of his staying in PNG until December and just meeting up in Australia for the wedding, but we decided that that was too mail-order-spouse even for us. So we've been based in the same city for the past four months.

Well, minus the two weeks I was in Africa for work. Oh, and a quick trip I took to D.C.

In a year full of good decisions, same-city living for a couple of months before the wedding was one of the best. It has let Mike get reacquainted with America after seven years away and given us shared experiences – decorating a Christmas tree, premarital counseling, learning that we have very different conceptions of what constitutes a "fun hike." Living in the same place has colored in between some of those lines we sketched out over Skype. The vast majority of those discoveries have been deliciously fun. Others, well …

"I don't get it," Mike said to me just six days ago at Los Angeles Airport. We were about to board the plane that would take us to Fiji and then on to Brisbane. I was carrying my wedding dress. It was the start of what I fully expected would become one of the happiest weeks of my life, and I was in the mood that commonly afflicts me in airports, frazzled and petulant.

"I don't get it," Mike repeated. "You're such a centered, rational, cheerful person most of the time. And then you walk into an airport and become someone completely different."

"Two words for you," I said. "*Cumulative stress*. I've been flying like this since I was seven years old. I hate airports and all the noise and immigration officers who never know what they're talking about and being squished up next to people on planes—"

"I still cannot believe that you booked yourself an aisle seat and me a window seat for our flight to New Zealand *for our honeymoon*."

"Oh please," I said. "This way we're much more likely to have a seat spare on our row. If someone gets put in the middle, one of us will just switch with them."

"That's not the *point*," Mike said. "It's our *honeymoon*. I want to sit next to you on the plane, regardless."

"We'll have plenty of time in New Zealand to sit next to each other," I said, unapologetic.

I wonder how long we will have been married before Mike decides that he really *doesn't* want to sit next to me on planes?

Now it's the day before the wedding. This morning I'm sitting on the side porch of the house, in the sun, looking out to sea over the laptop screen. The feathery leaves of the nearby poinciana tree are casting a delicate and wavery shade in the tease of the breeze. Clouds are scurrying around up there, storms threatening, as they will again tomorrow. This morning I went into the study to check the weather report and was a little disheartened to see "thunderstorms possible" listed next to the date of my wedding.

"Oh it's worse than that," Mum said cheerfully when I mentioned this over breakfast. "The report I checked said 'thunderstorms likely all day.'"

I'm a bit anxious about this, and a bit upset that I'm anxious. I want to be the sort of person who is unruffled by the prospect of rain on her wedding day. I want to be cheerfully adaptable. But I have to admit that I really *do* hope it doesn't rain on my wedding day. Not when we're getting married in the garden. Outside. And having our reception in a tent.

"I bought you this just in case it *does* rain," Mum said, almost as an afterthought, darting into the dinning room and coming back with an enormous, vibrant and multicolored golf umbrella.

Just looking at this umbrella made me feel better. It may well not go as we have hoped and planned tomorrow. It may well rain. But we will have a rainbow-colorful umbrella that screams *happy* and will look great in photographs.

Despite the storms that threaten, I'm glad we decided to get married here. I've never lived here – Mum and Dad have lived here only six years themselves. But here is the place I've been coming to relax, regroup, and re-connect with myself for years. Here, the place where Mike and I first got to know one another face-to-face. Here, the place of green grass, crimson flowers, sugar-cane fields, river, beach, and the dense inscrutable blue of the Pacific Ocean – all spread out in front of me as a feast. Here is about as close to a place called home as I can get.

———— ❦ ————

HOME HAS BEEN MORE about people than place to me for a long time now, but what I'm still learning is that it can't be all about people, either.

As recently as three months ago I forgot this yet again.

We wanted to write our own wedding vows, Mike and I, and we also wanted to be in sync with what we would promise each other on the day. So we each put some thought into the vows separately and then came together with our drafts to blend them into one unified declaration.

I think my favorite section of our vows is what we settled on for the ring exchange: "As I give you this ring, I give you my heart as a sanctuary. I give you myself as a faithful companion to celebrate life with. I give you my promise that as I choose you today, so I will choose you tomorrow. This is our covenant."

To get to these four simple sentences, we each had to make a compromise that initially felt quite painful.

"We can't say it that way," Mike said when he saw my draft. "The second sentence ends with a preposition."

"What's a preposition?" I asked.

Mike looked at me, suspicious.

"*You,*" he said, "are a *novelist*. How can you *possibly* not know what a preposition is?"

"Hey," I said a trifle sharply. "Six countries. Six schools. English grammar got lost somewhere along the way, possibly while I was busy learning Shona in Zimbabwe."

"You can't end a sentence with the word *with,*" Mike said. "It's just wrong. Another way to say it would be 'I give you myself as a faithful companion with whom to celebrate life.'"

"That sounds *lame*," I said, displaying a vocabulary every bit as impressive as my grasp on grammar.

"Well, at least it's correct."

"But it *sounds* dumb," I said. "Clumsy. Formal. It doesn't fit the tone of the rest of our vows. Who cares if it's correct if it sounds dumb?"

Mike eventually shifted on that issue and I shifted on this one: When I first drafted this section, I put an extra sentence in there. That sentence was "You will be home to me."

"I don't like that," Mike said when he saw it. "It doesn't work."

I was initially disappointed, but there was something in me that sensed he might just be right, so I took it out without making too much of a fuss, and now that I've had a couple of weeks to mull it over, I do think he was right after all. For one thing, that phrase is arguably less a promise than it is a statement, or even a demand.

I hadn't intended that. I had intended that sentence to evoke all that is most positive in the ideal of home – comfort, continuity, understanding, haven, refuge, rest, encouragement, wholeness – the sum total of all that is most precious and valuable in life. I had intended it as a promise along the lines of "I will seek these things in you, for you, and with you."

The problem here lies in the first part of that promise that I was trying to craft, the idea that it's possible to find all of that *in* someone else. It's too much to expect (or even hope for) from any one person, even your lover. It's too much to expect from other people altogether.

Don't get me wrong, I do think people are key. Relationships are primary, perhaps even central, to the concept of home. It's always been people who granted the most meaning and emotional heft to place for me, not the other way around. The happiest times of my life have been steeped in my richest community experiences. They had far less to do with where I was than with who was there with me.

I am reminded of a day several years ago when I was returning to L.A. from Amsterdam after a string of work trips. I was exhausted and dazed in that way that I get after too many sterile announcements about seat belts, life jackets, baggage carousels, and what color sign you can find the ride-share vans under. Familiarity is not always a good thing, and Los Angeles Airport is a case in point. It is one place where repetition has definitely *not* bred the happy emotional resonance we all want to associate with home. I dislike that airport with a passion that is rather unreasonable in magnitude and intensity.

That day, however, I didn't have to drag myself through collecting my bags or endure a circuitous shared ride back to my apartment. That day, when I came down the escalators near baggage claim, four familiar faces were waiting. They'd figured out which plane I would be on and decided to surprise me at the airport. They greeted me with homemade signs that read, "Welcome home!" and, "There's no place like home!!" And suddenly I *was* home in that moment, even in that airport, because they were there.

But friends and family are only part of the puzzle of home. They are the biggest and most important part, I do believe, but still only part. There is another level to home, a level where other people, no matter how close and loving, have only so much access and impact. A level everyone ultimately plumbs alone.

———∞∞∞———

THE WORD *HOME* COMES from a root meaning "the place where one lies." The phrase refers to our physical place of residence and rest, our bed, but it also prompts me to consider where the core of the "one" that is me – who I am, my soul – lies. It makes me think of identity, purpose, passion, and being at home in my own skin.

This one is a work in progress.

Last night my sister and girlfriends organized a little pre-wedding girls night. There were eight of us, Champagne, chocolate, strawberries, some practical pajamas, some not-so-practical saucy red lingerie, lots of chatter, and a surprise videotape.

Two of my bridesmaids, Tash and Ani, had decided that since none of my friends had met Mike more than once and therefore had quite a limited basis for deciding whether to give this marriage their stamp of approval, perhaps it might be a good idea to concoct a test to see how in sync Mike and I are with each other. So they cornered Mike with a video camera, asked him a long list of questions, and taped his responses. Then they brought this video to the party and played it bit by bit, stopping at the appropriate places (after they'd asked a question and before Mike answered) to make me guess what his answer would be.

This might *sound* like a bit of lighthearted fun, but those two went to town with their questions. They were hard!

What first attracted you to Lisa?

What do you like most about Lisa?

What do you think Lisa likes most about *you*?

That was just the warm-up. In fourteen minutes of footage they also covered what physical attributes of mine Mike likes the most and which of his he thinks I like? Ideal travel destinations? How many kids, if any, do we both want? How does Mike feel about my writing essays about the trials and tribulations of married life? If he were on a hike with me and I decided I'd had enough, sat down, and refused to go on, what would he do? What does Mike think of my driving, my cooking, and my house-cleaning? What is my favorite color? What really turns me on?

Mike was calm, composed and a perfect gentleman (except when he said that although he chose to believe that I was *capable* of house-cleaning, he had yet to see any evidence that this was true). The only time he looked completely panicked was when he was asked about my favorite color.

"What's Lisa's favorite color?" Mike repeated, laughing and bewildered. "I have no idea. *Por favor*! Is it … uh … uh …"

"This is a bonus question for bonus points," Tash taunted him from off-screen.

"Did she put it in any essays?" Mike said. "How am I supposed to know Lisa's favorite color? Um … is it … blue?"

Wrong. Favorite-color fail.

But I was both heartened and a little relieved to see that we *are* pretty much in sync on most of the other questions. I didn't know what Mike was going to pinpoint as what he likes most about me, but this is what he said: "I like most Lisa's confidence in who she is and how she approaches the world around her, wishing to engage in it and striving to respond to others as she is able."

Quite apart from the fact that my heart melted faster than butter under an equatorial sun listening to him say this, it was encouraging. When I think about being at home in my own skin, I think of confidence – a confidence that springs from exercising your strengths, understanding what you value, and having a clear sense of purpose.

Purpose is something Mike and I have spent a lot of time talking about. In the letters we exchanged before we met for the first time in Australia, we used the word *purpose* forty-two times. It is something that I'm still getting a handle on in my own life, and something I don't think should ever harden into something immutable. But there have been several grindstones that have contributed to the sharpening of my own sense of purpose during the last five years. Work has been one such grindstone, writing another, faith a third. I'm far less sure of the semantics of faith than I was a decade ago. The language of church doesn't fit me completely, and unshakable certainty in any domain scares me. But I do believe that I am part of a meaningful story that's far bigger and more important than just my own thread, and I believe that the heart of God is love.

Purpose. Passion. Meaning.

Without some baseline sense of these in your life, you may feel at home some places, or with some people, but you won't ever feel fully at home in yourself.

AFTER MIKE PROPOSED AND before he left for PNG again at the end of May, we talked engagement rings. Or, rather, we talked the framework of budget, since I didn't really have a clue what I wanted.

After he left, I had no idea where to start looking.

I thought I *would* quite like a ring of some sort, but I wasn't at all sure I wanted a diamond. I thought I might like an opal. Not a white one – they've always seemed rather milky and boring – but a black opal. There's something fascinating about how vivid fragments of blue, green, gold and red show up all fleeting and fiery in the depths of that dark stone. Black opals that are mostly blue and green look like earth as viewed from the moon – mysterious, magical, fecund.

It turns out, though, that opals bear one more similarity to planet Earth: they are quite fragile and prone to scratching and chipping if knocked about. So in the end I gave up on the idea of opals and returned to diamonds. After four months of engagement, three trips to Robbins Brothers, two changes of mind, and a partridge in a pear tree, I finally decided on an engagement ring. Two weeks after Mike arrived in Los Angeles in September we went to finalize the transaction.

"We just bought a small car for your finger," Mike said on the way home, shell-shocked.

"Well, yes. A small secondhand, car," I said and added quickly, "but it will be *much* more beautiful than a car."

There was an extended pause.

"At least this won't lose value like an actual car would," I said. "That could come in handy."

"How's that?" Mike asked.

"Well, you know, we might need to barter it for something someday," I said. "Like safe passage on a boat during a military coup."

There was another extended pause.

"I cannot believe you said that less than ten minutes after I signed the bill," Mike said.

"I would take you with me on the boat," I said.

"This is one of those times when you should just stop talking," Mike said.

"Hey!" I said. "I was *trying* to save your life."

"Yet all I can see is all the dirt flying out of that hole you're digging there," Mike said.

I decided to stop talking until I figured out whether Mike was actually upset. I was still trying to figure it out when we got back to my place fifteen minutes later.

Six weeks later the ring was ready and we went to pick it up. When they opened the box I was silent with awe. I had been right – it *was* much more beautiful than a car. Mike looked at it thoughtfully.

"Wow," he said. "It's really pretty. I'm going to miss it when we have to barter it for boat tickets."

I've never been much of a ring person, so I've been somewhat surprised by how much I love my engagement ring. After not even being sure I wanted one diamond, I ended up choosing a ring with three of them – a stone in the center flanked by two smaller ones. I love the delicacy of it, the symmetry, the sparkle as all those facets bounce light at me.

A single-faceted diamond wouldn't shine in nearly the same way, and perhaps that's a little like home. Place, people, purpose – those are all large, important facets in the lodestone of home. So is safety. So is familiarity in any loved form, and feeling understood and accepted and a contented sort of cozy. In between those defining planes, life has engraved dozens of other smaller facets on my own unique vision of home. They form a mélange of memory and sensation that can momentarily wink up at me, beautiful.

The feeling that comes when I write something that sings.

The message and the music of the song *Amazing Grace*.

The porch swing on the back deck of this house. My blue couch in L.A. In Mike's arms.

Jacaranda flowers. Great books. Flannel pajamas.

Warm, slippery mango. A grassy sauvignon blanc. Takeout Indian on the beach. Chili barbecued prawns. Orange chicken and chow mein. My grandmother's passion-fruit sponge cake.

The smell of salt water, wood smoke, eucalyptus, mosquito repellant, diesel fuel, jasmine.

The plangent chime of my engagement ring landing in the

Turkish pottery bowl on my bedside table when I take it off at night.

———— ∞ ————

I, LISA MCKAY, CHOOSE you, Michael Wolfe, as my life partner, the one I commit to love. I pledge to cherish and honor you regardless of circumstances, in the pressures of the present and the uncertainties of the future, loving what I do know of you, trusting what I do not yet know.

I promise to grow in mind and spirit with you, and support you in fulfilling your hopes and dreams. I promise to remain with you, whatever afflictions may befall. I commit to sharing with you life's joys and sorrows, pleasures and pains from this day forward until death do us part.

———— ∞ ————

I AM GOING TO put on a beautiful dress tomorrow and walk down a grassy aisle littered with frangipanis to the celestial sounds of *Gabriel's Oboe* from *The Mission*. And then I will make these promises.

In the end I am not going to promise or demand that Mike will be home to me – after a certain point in life, perhaps home is more something you make than something you have, anyway. But I will, in essence, be promising to fashion a home *with* him.

I have no idea what places, people, and purposes that will come to mean.

This scares the part of me that longs for the white-picket-fence version of home, that wants to predict and control the future and that yearns for the grounding grace of routine. It thrills the part of me that longs for the sharp spur of purpose to drive me from my comfort zone, that craves the cold-shower shock of novelty and the adventures of dirt roads less traveled. I'm not

sure that these paradoxical longings will ever be fully reconciled
– I'm no longer sure that's even the point. I am, however, certain
that I want Mike to be beside me whatever form home might
take for me in the future. I am convinced that a white picket
fence with him would be better than bumping down a dirt road
without him and that traveling a dirt road together would beat
out a white picket fence that's mine alone. That sort of peaceful
surety is worth following down an aisle and across the world,
don't you think?

I do.

ACKNOWLEDGEMENTS

AS USUAL, WRITING THIS book has been a longer and more challenging journey than I had anticipated. Many people have supported and encouraged me along the way. I especially want to thank …

All the wonderful strangers who posted online reviews after reading *my hands came away red* and wrote me letters sharing their thoughts and asking when my next book would be coming out.

Andy McGuire for calling *Hands* my "first novel" – words that forced me to explore the possibility of a second book.

Chip MacGregor for believing in the big picture of me as a writer, for providing helpful input on the first draft, for championing this book and for tracking with my story.

Jennifer Anthony, Lisa Borden, Tristan Clements, Leah Curtis, Sarah Kelly, Andy McGuire, Chip MacGregor, Lloyd McKay, Merrilyn McKay, Hilary Reed, Janet Shriberg, Erica Sloan, Natasha White, and Michelle Williams for reading the first draft and providing much useful feedback and encouragement to keep going.

Joslyne Decker and Amy Lyles Wilson for their invaluable and detailed input on the second draft.

Fellow authors Nicole Baart, Leeana Tankersley, Susan Meissner, Gina Holmes, Lisa Samson, Torre DeRoche and Lisa Borden for their encouragement and input.

Ryan for being casually good humored when I emailed him a draft of this book and admitted I had e-stalked him.

Jason for being gracious and transparent when I emailed him a draft of this book and admitted that I had treated him less than well.

My parents, Lloyd and Merrilyn McKay, and my siblings,

Matthew McKay and Michelle Williams, for letting me share snippets of their lives and for being such important parts of mine.

Everyone else who appears in these pages. You have all touched my life deeply.

In particular, Michael Wolfe. For writing that first email and so many more since. For being such a thoughtful and caring partner. For reading every draft and for all the other ways in which you encourage me to follow my passions. For daring to tell me that the first draft was "a good start that needed a lot more work" and for spending time with our precious baby when you can so that I can have some uninterrupted writing time. Three years down the track, I would choose you again without hesitating.

AUTHOR'S NOTE

DEAR READER,

Thank you so much for spending time with me by reading this book. If you enjoyed it, please consider leaving a review on Amazon, Barnes and Noble, GoodReads or other book forums.

Mike and I have been married for three years now. A lot has happened during those three years – not least of which is a baby and a move. We're currently living in Luang Prabang, Laos.

If you'd like to find out more or stop by and say hello, please visit www.lisamckaywriting.com. I would love to hear from you!

Lisa
June 2012

READING GROUP GUIDE

Topics and questions for discussion

HOME

1. Throughout the book, Lisa ponders the concept of home. What are some of the words and places she associates with home? What conclusions does she eventually come to about home?
2. Lisa and Mike write about "the internal and unwinnable war between the longing for adventure and home." Do you feel that Adventure and Home necessarily stand in opposition to each other?
3. What do you associate with the word *home*? What are some of your earliest memories of home?

TRAVEL AND CHANGE

1. Lisa travels a lot. What are some of the gifts this travel gives her? What are some of the costs?
2. How have your own travels helped you see the world differently?
3. Lisa asks herself this question: "At what point does a constant stream of change *blunt* our ability to feel and connect to the present and to ourselves?" What do you think? What are some other things that blunt your ability to feel and connect to the present and yourself?

ALTERNATIVE LIVES

1. How did Lisa feel about turning 30? Have you struggled with any of your birthdays? Why?
2. In *Alternate Lives,* Lisa says: "The basic economic

principle of opportunity cost holds just as true in relation to the wealth of time as it does for money. By choosing this, I am giving up other lives – different lives that would shape a different me." Do you daydream about an alternate life for yourself? What do your alternative lives look like?

3. In *Spinsters Abroad,* Lisa says: "I am starting to catch myself wondering … whether … I'll wake up in fifteen years and still believe that it was worth it – this choice that I have made again and again throughout my twenties to pursue adventure and novelty and helping people in faraway lands rather than stability and continuity and helping people in a land I claim as mine." Are you making a choice like this – a choice you wonder whether you'll still believe it was worth it in the future?

LOVE

1. In *The Shadow of the Golden Dome* Lisa writes believing that love was more of a campfire than a lightening bolt. Do you believe in love at first sight?

2. In *Chasing Silver Dollars,* Lisa writes, "A soul mate, I believed, would meet me on a visceral, darker level. He would have an instinctive understanding, borne out of experience, of the elements that made up my own particular potpourri of angst – constant change, the guilt of privilege, too much witnessed suffering, a battle between hope and cynicism, and a search for God that wouldn't let you rest even during times when you weren't at all sure you believed in God. There would be the companionship of keenly felt questions." Do you believe soul mates exist? What makes a soul mate for you?

3. Do you think that Lisa could have handled the situation

with Jason and Ryan better? How? What lessons have you learned from your own misjudgments in previous relationships?

4. What are some of the benefits and pitfalls of long distance relationships?

5. In *Shock and Awe In Love*, Lisa asks: "Just how sure did I need to be to make a commitment of this magnitude?" What do you think? How do *you* know when to say yes or no in crucial moments?

FAITH, HOPE AND PASSION

1. In *The Internal and Unwinnable War*, Mike asks Lisa this question: "How have your ideas about faith changed over the past 10ish years? How have your ideas about faith expanded and contracted as you've come face-to-faith with tragedies of human existence and as you've encountered people from different cultures and worldviews and faith walks?" How did she answer it? How would you?

2. In *Hope Chases Us*, Lisa and Mike write to each other about hope and passion. What makes you feel hopeful? What about passionate?

A COUPLE OF EXTRAS

1. What role has reading played in Lisa's life? What role has it played in yours?

2. What do you think about the way that Lisa handled the situation with Travis? Have you ever encountered a situation where you expect mental illness was involved? If so, how did you handle it?

3. Do fairytales exist in "real life"?

Thank you for reading! If you enjoyed this book please consider leaving a short review on Amazon, Barnes and Noble, GoodReads or other book forums.

Visit www.lisamckaywriting.com for more, including the free e-book *201 Great Discussion Questions for Couples in Long Distance Relationships.*

Also by Lisa McKay
My Hands Came Away Red